Digital Exiles

Digital Exiles

Refugee Work in the Global Digital Economy

Andreas Hackl

The MIT Press
Cambridge, Massachusetts | London, England

The MIT Press
Massachusetts Institute of Technology
77 Massachusetts Avenue
Cambridge, MA 02139
mitpress.mit.edu

The open access edition of this book was made possible by generous funding from the Economic and Social Research Council (ESRC).

The MIT Press would like to thank the anonymous peer reviewers who provided comments on drafts of this book. The generous work of academic experts is essential for establishing the authority and quality of our publications. We acknowledge with gratitude the contributions of these otherwise uncredited readers.

This book was set in Stone Serif and Stone Sans by Westchester Publishing Services. Printed and bound in the United States of America.

Library of Congress Cataloging-in-Publication Data is available.

ISBN: 978-0-262-05245-0

EU Authorised Representative: Easy Access System Europe, Mustamäe tee 50, 10621 Tallinn, Estonia | Email: gpsr.requests@easproject.com

Contents

Acknowledgments

Writing a monograph after many years of individual and collaborative research offers an opportunity to further develop the contributions and insights that earlier publications offered. At the same time, this monograph remains firmly grounded in the research, creative thinking, and collaborative writing that preceded it. The long and fruitful journey behind this book formally started with the award of a New Investigator Grant by the Economic and Social Research Council (ESRC) in the UK, which allowed me to fully dedicate myself to research for two years (2019–2021). Here I am indebted to the contributions of the two excellent researchers I worked with: Watfa Najdi conducted a large part of the research in Lebanon and coauthored a journal article with me that provided the basis for developing the Lebanon chapter in this book, and Philip Rushworth conducted a significant part of the research in Berlin while coauthoring a journal article that formed the basis for another of the book's chapters. During this ESRC-funded project, I enjoyed the mentorship of Jamie Cross at the University of Edinburgh and Mark Graham at the Oxford Internet Institute, where I spent three productive months as a visiting postdoctoral fellow.

Throughout this initial two-year project and the subsequent years of research and collaboration, the success of my work benefited from many individuals and organizations. In Lebanon, I was lucky to have enjoyed the support of Rabih Shibli, Sarah Kouzi, and Brooke Atherton El-Amine at the Center for Civic Engagement and Community Service at the American University of Beirut, whose efforts have done so much to support digital skills training in the country. In Berlin, our research was made possible by the team of the ReDI School of Digital Integration and the openness of their volunteers and program beneficiaries. The research behind this book further benefited from the support and trust of all the inspiring individuals who have worked tirelessly to support refugees through digital skills training and employment: the team of Humans in the Loop, especially Hester Gartrell, Tess Valbuena, Iva Gumnishka, and Zoe Holliday; Aline Sara and the team behind NaTakallam; Karina Grosheva and the enterprise TaQadam; the team behind the Digital Opportunity Trust and the impact sourcing platform B.O.T.; and Frida Mwangi at iWorkers Kenya. Moreover, I am grateful for the collaboration and friendship with the researcher and entrepreneur Lorraine Charles, who founded and directed Na'amal, and whose seemingly infinite energy and dedication has made so many good things possible for refugees. Beyond the few I can name here, there have been numerous other individuals and initiatives that have engaged with the research behind this book along the way. Above all, I am indebted to all the participants who were motivated to engage with this research and took some time out of their busy lives to speak with me and my research collaborators.

In the wider academic research community, I am thankful for all the exchanges, collaborations, and friendships that made the research and the writing for this book not only worthwhile but also enjoyable. I would like to thank Evan Easton-Calabria for enriching conversations and our fruitful collaboration in publishing, as well as Margie Cheesman for her support and friendship and for being an excellent collaborator in organizing events and publications. Additional thanks go to all my colleagues at the University of Edinburgh and especially to those who helped me develop the original idea into a successful research project, including Juli Huang, Ann-Christin Zuntz, Karen Gregory, and Guido Sanguinetti. Moreover, I am grateful for the continuous support I received by my former PhD supervisor and mentor Toby Kelly as I progressed through the different stages of my academic career.

The original research project I started in 2019 further enabled me to initiate a collaboration with the ILO that continued for many years and took on different shapes. Initially, the collaboration was made possible by the kind support and enthusiasm of Christiane Kuptsch, Senior Specialist in Migration Policies at the ILO's Labour Migration Branch. Here, I am deeply thankful for the opportunity to present the project at an early stage at the ILO's headquarters in Geneva and for the support in publishing the ILO report *Digital Refugee Livelihoods and Decent Work*. Thanks to this collaboration, I then had the opportunity to contribute research and expertise as an external collaborator to a project commissioned by the ILO's Employment, Labour Markets, and Youth Branch under the "Partnership for improving prospects for forcibly displaced persons and host communities" (PROSPECTS). With the guidance of Drew Gardiner and Susana Porto, this led to the publication of the ILO report titled *Towards Decent Work for Young Refugees and Host Communities in the Digital Platform Economy in Africa: Kenya, Uganda, Egypt.*

This collaboration later allowed me to contribute expertise and research to a joint ILO-UNHCR project titled "Promotion, Inclusion and Protection of Refugees in the Gig Economy: Realizing Rights at Work and Mitigating Digital Risk." Important experience and knowledge for this book was gained by directing ILO-commissioned research at the University of Edinburgh, which explored the opportunities and challenges a digital economy poses for forcibly displaced people across eight countries in the Middle East and Africa (Kenya, Uganda, Ethiopia, Sudan, Iraq, Egypt, Lebanon, and Jordan). At the ILO, I am grateful for the support and guidance of Zulum Avila and Nick Grisewood and for the patient rounds of report editing by Nicolás Díaz Castellanos. Special thanks go to the research team behind this tremendous effort, including contributions in desk-based research and coauthorships of reports by Zeineb Alsabeegh, Clayton Boeyink, Júlia Fernandez Molina, David Mesa-Ruiz, Alec Ross, Vicente Silva, and Oyku Hazal Tural. Additional research was conducted by consultants at Samuel Hall. Although the data generated by this research primarily contributed to reports that we submitted to the ILO, the long journey of working and thinking with these talented researchers inevitably also helped me shape the ideas and insights that make up this book.

Additional collaboration with UNHCR's Innovation Service became possible thanks to the kind support and trust of John Warnes, who welcomed me as an external collaborator during a short consultancy and was then instrumental in realizing a small project with funding from an ESRC Impact Accelerator Account grant. This enabled Margie Cheesman and me to jointly run a series of workshops on the many risks refugees faced in the digital economy, including a workshop with focus group discussions in Nairobi, Kenya. Many thanks to John for having been the best possible host in Nairobi, and for having co-organized the workshop there. Additional thanks go to the livelihoods team at the UNHCR office in Kenya, and especially Meshack Mwololo for cohosting the workshop, and to the teams and beneficiaries of the organizations RefuSHE, WUSC, Cohere, and Konnexio, who participated in the workshop.

The combined experience of academic research and applied work with practitioners inspired me to seek a healthy balance between the book's academic rigorousness and the accessibility of its writing. The hope is that the following pages will be useful and engaging both for experts and for a wider general readership interested in this topic. The quality of the final book ultimately benefited from the valuable input that two anonymous reviewers provided. I am equally grateful for the MIT Press editors who took the book project under contract at a very early stage and remained committed to it despite several delays. One of these delays was at least for a very good reason: the birth of my son Rowan in 2023. Finally, and perhaps most importantly, I would like to thank my partner Kate for supporting me throughout the long journey that led up to this book's publication, for always believing in my work, and for freeing up important time and space for me during the final revision period.

Introduction

Refugees in the Global Digital Economy

Digitalization is rapidly changing the experience of work around the world. For many of the world's refugees, this change offers promising new opportunities for employment and income generation. Consider the growing number of forcibly displaced people who are encouraged to become online freelance workers in places such as Kenya's Dadaab Refugee Complex. In one of the world's largest camps, where some 420,000 people live in basic huts or makeshift shelters,[1] refugees work remotely as translators and writers through digital labor platforms where they sell their services to paying clients all over the world. Digital jobs and remote work have also provided a lifeline to people who are affected by economic and humanitarian crisis. In Lebanon, where 90 percent of some 1.5 million Syrian refugees have faced extreme poverty,[2] training programs supported a small minority of refugees and Lebanese youth to supplement their income with digital and remote work in fields such as data entry, image classification, and online language teaching. Even in high-income countries such as Germany, Syrian refugees who attended coding schools in the city of Berlin have welcomed the digital economy as a more inclusive alternative to traditional sectors of the labor market.

The opportunity to learn digital skills and thereby enter a digital economy has helped build bridges across the economic, geographic, and legal limitations that affect many of the 122 million forcibly displaced people around the world.[3] Remote work can virtually cross the boundaries of refugee camps even if people are forced to stay put. Online freelance work on transnational digital platforms can bypass bureaucratic barriers and regulations that restrict refugees' access to employment in the labor markets of host countries. Digital careers and coding jobs are being promoted as a shortcut to employment for refugees and migrants, seemingly enabled by the boundary-crossing and hypermobile capabilities of digital technology. These developments suggest that the global spread of a digital economy holds vast potential for job creation among refugees. At the same time, the majority of forcibly displaced people remain locked out of these opportunities and inhabit the extreme margins of a digital economy. Those few who benefit from digital livelihood opportunities are being exposed to many new challenges and risks that result from the growing roles that digital inclusion and connectivity play in their lives. Scrutinizing the promises of digital economic liberation from the viewpoint of refugees reveals a tension between this powerful imaginary and the difficult reality they face on the ground: Just as digital jobs and remote work are enthusiastically promoted as a magical quick fix to some of the challenges they face, most refugees continue to experience digital transformation as a sobering reality of digital divides, systematic exclusion, job precarity, and newly emerging risks. As a Syrian software developer in the city of Berlin told me, "In the media, there is often this feeling that digital is the solution, that digital integration is a solution. It sounds cool and good. But it doesn't really work, or at least it's not a magical thing."

The Digital Economy and Refugee Livelihoods

The wider *digital economy* broadly incorporates all kinds of economic activity that is reliant on, or significantly enhanced by, digital technologies, digital infrastructures, and data.[4] In this book, I approach the digital economy through two main dimensions: work and jobs that use digital means and create digital products, such as software programming, data entry, and web design; and remote work that is mediated by digital platforms but not necessarily digital in nature, such as language services or translation. The notion of *digital livelihoods* refers to the wider field of international development and humanitarian practice that aims to leverage this digital economy to support refugees' livelihoods and contribute to their economic self-reliance. Digital livelihood programs commonly involve digital skills training courses and other mechanisms of support that are designed to overcome barriers and build bridges between beneficiaries and a digital economy.[5]

The gradual emergence of digital refugee livelihoods as a field of development and humanitarian aid is rooted in the confluence of two major global transformations: the growing digitalization of work and a steep rise in forced displacement. At a time when the number of forcibly displaced people doubled to more than 122 million in just over a decade, including some 38 million refugees and 8 million asylum seekers,[6] the number of digital platforms connecting workers to businesses and clients grew by some 450 percent over a 13-year period.[7] Workers around the world are told, "Acquire digital skills or get left behind." Online work and digital jobs offer a powerful promise that seems tailor-made for evading the restrictions to mobility and employment many refugees face. Coding schools promote digital skills as a shortcut to a new career for migrants and refugees who struggle to find good jobs in a new unfamiliar country. Digital platforms offer a seeming abundance of remote work opportunities in fields ranging from basic data entry to advanced software development and language translation. Just as coding schools often suggest that anyone who puts in the work can become a successful computer programmer, online freelancing platforms convey the idea that *anyone* from *anywhere* can make money remotely. These powerful assumptions suggest a pathway to success and freedom, one that is epitomized by widespread images of "digital nomads" who work from cafés and beaches in desirable locations. Could the growing numbers of refugees who are being trained to work as online freelancers and IT experts become a new kind of digital nomad in this sense?

The problem is that refugees are not *anyone* and they do not live *anywhere*. Who they are and where they live influences their ability to benefit from digital jobs and remote work. They often encounter obstacles outside their control that undermine their ability to earn money from digital and remote work.[8] Unlike the romanticized figure of the digital nomad, forcibly displaced people do not usually enjoy the freedom to move to and live in a location of their choice. Many live crowded into refugee camps that lack reliable internet connectivity and suitable workspaces. Those who live in rural areas of developing countries do not have fixed internet connectivity, and mobile broadband is often weak and expensive. Some 71 percent of refugees were hosted in low- and middle-income countries by 2025,[9] where refugees tend to face significant barriers to digital inclusion and formal employment. The refugees who are hosted in high-income countries can equally face significant challenges on their way into a digital economy, including a lack of digital skills and difficulties to afford mobile data, computers, and smartphones.

Being forcibly displaced and uprooted from a homeland also makes it harder for people to access education and develop the necessary skills to flourish in a digital world of work. Even for those who are digitally connected and have strong skill sets, a myriad of barriers abounds: Without recognized identification documents such as passports or national IDs, they can be prevented from registering SIM cards and cannot open bank accounts or digital platform accounts. Some nationalities are blocked from using digital platforms and financial services because of international sanctions against their home countries and the very political regimes they escaped. Refugees searching for jobs locally and remotely also face discrimination based on their identity and status while also running the risk of being exploited through underpaid work and unpaid traineeships. A growing number of refugees are targeted by scams and cybercriminals who take advantage of their vulnerabilities and desperation.

As if these problems were not enough, connecting refugees to some digital jobs exposes them to potentially precarious working conditions without security of income, access to social protection, and rights at work.[10] This is especially true for online gig work that is mediated by digital labor platforms, where self-employed workers compete for jobs and gigs in a global labor market. The majority of workers on these remote work platforms are based in the Global South and many face discrimination based on their location or nationality.[11] The working arrangements on these platforms feature uncertainty, frequently low pay and unpaid labor time, fierce competition, long working hours, and a range of risks to people's mental health and well-being.[12] Such work is hardly ideal for refugees fleeing wars and other crises, whose lives are already fraught with uncertainty and risk. Although learning digital skills can help some refugees find formal employment, this prospect is largely reserved for a minority of highly educated people who live in countries with enabling policies and a high demand for digitally skilled workers.

Despite many barriers and risks, the digital economy continues to represent an "aspirational sector" that refugees are determined to shift toward.[13] Refugee-serving organizations and programs in this field often encourage such a shift, emphasizing the need for refugees not only to build skills but also to shift their "mindset" if they aspire to succeed in the digital economy. As they promote self-employed digital work, organizations and "tech for good" enterprises intensify a long-standing marketization of refugee-serving aid in which entrepreneurship is seen as a pathway to self-reliance.[14] Digital and remote jobs have come to embody a new dream of self-reliance for people who are in desperate need of work and live in very challenging conditions, often with a restricted freedom to move. For refugees, the digital economy has become the "preserve of those with nowhere else to go."[15]

From Niche to Hype: The Emergence of a New Field

The topic of digital refugee economies sits in a narrow space between research on forced displacement and research on digital economies. When I first developed a research project on digital refugee livelihoods in 2017, the field still felt very niche and research only emerged slowly. This may have been the case because the phenomenon itself only started to take off: Most initiatives that promoted digital livelihoods for refugee self-reliance started in response to the mass displacement of Syrians in 2015 and 2016.[16] Early events that brought researchers and practitioners together to discuss insights from this field, such as a workshop of the United Nations Development Programme (UNDP) titled "Migrant Nation" in Geneva, felt like retreats of a small crowd of dedicated enthusiasts, as well as a handful of academics who observed with skepticism how this new world of enthusiasm unfolded. A report linked to the workshop offered a first mapping of digital skills training and digital livelihoods initiatives for refugees while critically discussing both the benefits and the challenges that digital work can bring to forcibly displaced people.[17]

Another early publication came out of a workshop I organized at the University of Edinburgh in 2019, focusing on migration and digital work. The edited collection published by the International Labour Organization (ILO) was titled *Digital Refugee Livelihoods and Decent Work* and advocated for a fairer digital economy for refugees, incorporating case study chapters authored by pioneering practitioners and researchers in the field. Contributions included research on digital skills training for refugees,[18] connectivity barriers and informal innovations among refugees living in camps,[19] gender dynamics in the refugee gig economy,[20] and the role of the private sector in hiring refugees remotely.[21] In addition to several practice-oriented reports on digital work and refugee livelihoods,[22] such as a major UN High Commissioner for Refugees (UNHCR)–funded study based on sixty-two community workshops with refugees in seven countries,[23] academic research directly focusing on refugee work in a digital economy also increasingly surfaced. There was a significant growth and diversification of topics from 2023 onward. These studies included research on the role of online and remote work in economic crises,[24] the spatial imaginaries attached to digital economies and its role in reinforcing inequalities affecting refugee women,[25] the digital "financial encampment" of refugees in humanitarian livelihood programs,[26] and the role of promoting gig work in wider efforts of enhancing refugee self-reliance.[27] Another innovative study examined the contemporary role of digital technology and digital economies for refugees living in cities.[28] The growing recognition of the field's significance was further underlined by a 2024 issue of the influential magazine *Forced Migration Review* titled "Digital Disruption and Displacement," which addressed key issues of digital refugee economies, such as the role of digital literacy[29] and the structural barriers refugees face in accessing the platform economy,[30] while discussing the wider potential and drawbacks of digital refugee livelihoods.[31]

Wider research on the digital platform economy has also increasingly recognized the specific role of digital jobs for migrant populations, including those who are forcibly displaced.[32] Part of this has been a gradual "platformization" of low-wage migratory labor markets through their incorporation into gig work and digitally mediated jobs.[33] The gradual growth of new research was paralleled by the rapid spread of programs and initiatives that promoted digital work and livelihoods among refugees from 2015 onward. All of this may have contributed to the recognition of refugees as a special category of platform workers in need of protection by the ILO.[34] The increasing evidence base about the barriers and risks that refugees can face in a digital world informed UNHCR's digital transformation strategy (2022–2026), which prioritizes digital inclusion and equitable access, protection from digital risks, and access to efficient and safe digital services.[35]

It is safe to say that almost all publications and applied programs recognize the potential of the digital economy for job creation among forcibly displaced people. Most of them also highlight the urgency of addressing the significant barriers and risks that can marginalize and even harm refugees in a digital world of work. Unfortunately, the pressing issue of creating an inclusive and fair digital economy for refugees has not been met with adequate responses by policymakers and the governments of refugee-hosting countries.

The gradual incorporation of more refugees into a quickly expanding digital economy has outpaced the policies and regulatory reforms that would be needed to protect workers and support those at risk of being left behind. In the absence of strong regulations, policies, and laws to mitigate risks for refugees and ensure decent working conditions, aid organizations and a variety of refugee-serving initiatives have struggled to fill this vacuum. In Germany, coding schools for refugees provide skills training, career counseling, mentoring, and traineeships for migrants and refugees who have been failed by the traditional labor market. In Lebanon, organizations and social enterprises have worked hard to equip a few thousand refugees with digital skills despite government restrictions in a small crisis-affected country that hosts the largest refugee population pre-capita in the world. In Kenya, initiatives tapped into the connective and boundary-crossing capabilities of online platform work to enable refugees who live in the confinement of camps to make a living.

Beyond these cases, similar efforts to include refugees and other marginalized populations in the digital economy have been underway in many other major refugee-hosting countries around the world, including in Least Developed Countries (LDCs) such as Uganda,[36] Ethiopia,[37] and Bangladesh,[38] as well as in Middle Eastern countries like Jordan,[39] Egypt,[40] Palestine,[41] Iraq,[42] and Turkey,[43] among others. Despite the significance of programs and initiatives that aim to create livelihood opportunities for refugees, most of the leading actors in this field have been unable to change the terms and conditions of work set out by major global platforms and digital labor markets, even as they connect refugees to these jobs and support them with skills and equipment.[44]

Discussions over whether the prevalence of precarious working conditions is an urgent problem or whether it is something to be solved in the future oscillate between a humanitarian standpoint and one rooted in development and labor rights: In the context of humanitarian assistance for displaced people who require immediate means to sustain their livelihood, access to precarious digital work may still be better than no income at all. But held against the benchmarks of labor rights and decent work standards, most jobs in the digital economy do not perform very well. Especially online gig work has contributed to further vulnerabilities and risks among refugee workers. One of the underlying problems is that self-employed platform workers and other freelancers face very high levels of informality that mirror the long-standing prevalence of insecure and informal refugee economies.[45] Whether or not such informality is a problem depends on the perspective.

Informality in the Digital Economy: Problem or Opportunity?

The informality of some digital jobs is a normative problem of eroding labor standards with real effects on people's lives. These effects are hardly a novelty for refugees who have long worked in insecure and informal jobs, especially in the Global South. Developing countries are not only where three-quarters of the world's refugees live but also where 93 percent of the world's informal employment is located.[46] The online gig economy now expands this long-standing trend. It gradually becomes a digital extension of the informal refugee economy. Sometimes, it is precisely the informality of web-based jobs that can evade bureaucracy and regulations and thereby make them appealing and accessible for refugees, especially for the 62 percent who live in countries with restricted access to formal employment within national labor markets.[47]

While online freelance work among refugees remains largely unregulated in most developing countries, national labor markets often feature strict regulations and rules for refugee employment overall. As a result, refugees arriving in a new country are often unable to have their qualifications recognized, can be prevented from working in certain sectors, and face bureaucratic obstacles and costs in obtaining work permits and new skills. Discrimination, language barriers, and other sociocultural challenges further undermine their integration into the labor markets of host countries. Many major refugee-hosting countries aim to prevent such integration altogether by crowding refugees into camps designed as temporary shelter, where they require permits to move elsewhere and are prevented from moving to the cities or towns where most jobs are. Three-quarters of refugees live in countries that restrict their freedom of movement.[48] By comparison, the idea of opening a computer to create a digital profile on a platform and start applying for remote jobs can instill powerful hopes and dreams of mobility in refugees who live with movement restrictions and spatial confinement. The same is true for refugees who cannot work in their previous jobs and take part in coding schools that promise to accelerate them into a new digital career within the Information and Communications Technology (ICT) sector of their host country. A vibrant tech sector in cities such as Berlin is widely perceived to be less formal, more diverse, and more inclusive than many jobs in traditional professions and sectors of the economy.[49]

Informality can therefore offer important opportunities for refugees, even as it also fosters precarity and insecurity. The underlying risks could be mitigated by more rights and protections for workers, which would in turn require more regulations and formal rules that hold platforms accountable. Yet, formalizing the digital economy can easily surface new problems despite the initial intention of improving the quality and security of jobs for workers. For example, the ILO sees the "traceability" of digital transactions in platform work as an opportunity to formalize economic activities that "are frequently hidden from the eye of the authorities."[50] Refugees and asylum seekers rarely feel a need to open the eyes of the authorities any further. They have also become highly suspicious of innovations that want to make their identity digitally recognized and more visible, partly for justified fears of data misuse and other negative consequences.[51] Those who live in countries with highly restricted access to employment could be excluded by new rules and regulations that seek to formalize online and remote work, especially if their right to work and start a business is not enshrined in law and exercised in practice. As some countries move to tax digital services, online freelance workers must register with the tax authorities, which can pose new barriers for asylum seekers and refugees with ambivalent legal statuses, or those without any official ID. As much as informality becomes a source of precarity and risk, formalities in the shape of regulations, rules, and laws become a key driver of refugees' exclusion from the digital economy. Persistent inequalities in connectivity and skills that maintain a rigid digital divide are yet another.

Refugees and the Digital Divide

Almost a third of humanity (2.6 billion people) remain offline, and around 96 percent of them are in developing countries. While internet usage is near universal in high-income countries, only 27 percent of people in low-income countries use the internet. Hundreds of millions more can only go online infrequently, often only through shared devices, or they have to use connectivity speeds that limit the usefulness of their devices. Similarly, while 3G and 4G coverage now theoretically covers 95 percent of the world population, only around half of people in developing countries are actually using mobile internet, and many in some of the poorest countries cannot connect due to high prices of devices and data costs relative to their income.[52] The digital divide includes not only barriers to connectivity and digital access but also inequalities that affect the usage and outcomes of technology use.[53]

This global digital divide affects forcibly displaced people in particularly severe ways: Even though many refugees are covered by mobile broadband networks and use mobile phones—and some even take part in digital skills programs—they often cannot afford connectivity and devices, cannot always register a SIM card due to a lack of recognized IDs, or are prevented from opening bank accounts and using the digital payment services needed to benefit from digital and remote jobs.[54] Moreover, refugees hosted in developing countries often live in rural areas or camps with weak and unreliable connectivity.[55]

With frequently disrupted and difficult-to-access education, refugees find further challenges in developing the competitive skills they need to compete for web-based income opportunities.[56] The digital economy is widening existing inequalities further because of a digital skills gap between those who can and those who cannot benefit from digital jobs and remote work opportunities. Despite the important work of coding schools and other training programs, refugees who seek employment in the digital economies of host countries must compete with highly qualified host community members and international talent. Moreover, the educational levels of workers on web-based digital labor platforms are very high: Some 60 percent of workers on major remote work platforms have university degrees, which rises to 73 percent among workers who are based in developing countries.[57] Most jobs demanded on major global freelancing platforms are in high-skill categories, including in the software development and technology category (39.3 percent), followed by creative and multimedia jobs (20.8 percent), with 12.2 percent in writing and translation and 11 percent in marketing and sales.[58] The biggest field of platform work on a lower-skill spectrum is clerical and data entry work, with a global share of 14 percent.[59]

One field of widely promoted refugee work on a lower-skill spectrum helps develop some of the world's most advanced digital technologies, such as artificial intelligence (AI). Here, individual workers annotate data and images to train AI models, often with the support of social impact platforms and enterprises. They have become an important part of the global human workforce that is hidden in the supply chains of AI. The adoption of AI in organizations and companies more than doubled from 2017 to 2022, and human inputs and annotations to train machine learning have been outsourced through major crowd-work platforms in the shape of small, disaggregated tasks. Conditions for these "microworkers" are particularly precarious, according to the Fairwork Foundation, which surveyed 250 platform workers in this field and found that they only made an average of US$2.15 per hour, had more than a quarter of their work time unpaid, and faced increasingly low rates for their work.[60] Data annotation tasks are subject to intensive competition over who offers both quality and the lowest price, with some critiques calling it "petty data work" that has been refashioned as "the latest saviour" to rescue marginalized populations and economies of the Global South.[61] As AI models are becoming more and more advanced and most data on the internet has already been scraped and used for training models, more highly paid and high-quality data training work for AI may soon become more prominent, as humans are no longer needed for the most basic tasks.[62] Social enterprises that source this kind of work for refugees increasingly come under pressure to provide more advanced, specialized, and high-quality work in a highly competitive market. Training programs come under pressure to equip refugees with more advanced skills. All of this happens at a time when major cuts in aid funding have severely affected the feasibility of costly development programs.

At the time of research for this book, basic data annotation and labeling jobs were still very prominent in refugee-serving initiatives because of the low skills threshold for entry and the relative ease with which new entrants could be prepared for a project. Unless they already have advanced skills that are in high demand, the majority of the world's refugees remain ill equipped to match the demand profiles of advanced digital careers and remote jobs. This is especially so for refugees hosted in low-income countries, which tend to have larger digital skills gaps and increased barriers to digital inclusion.[63] Barriers to connectivity and device ownership also make it difficult for many refugees to develop their skills independently, undermining the feasibility of making a web-based livelihood. For example, only 1.5 percent of Syrian refugee households in Lebanon reported in a UN survey that they had a computer at home.[64]

If we want to understand how the inequalities affecting refugees translate into digitally mediated divides, it is important to look beyond questions of access. Rather than merely being a question of exclusion, digital inequalities can be perpetuated through adverse incorporation into digital spaces: Poor and vulnerable populations may be able to access digital services, but in ways that commodify and exploit them to extract value,[65] while also placing them within second-class digital systems that lack key protections or features.[66] One example of a second-class system is digital wallets that refugees without official identity documents can access while only being allowed to use them with restricted functionalities, and often only because humanitarian organizations vouch for them. These emerging forms of digital and financial "encampment"[67] show that the very digital solutions designed to free displaced people from the restrictions they encounter in exile become inherently limited themselves. This contributes to a wider condition of digital exile that is characterized by a confluence of mobility and immobility, of opportunities and their foreclosure.

The Formation of Digital Exile

In the shadows of digital transformation, a new dimension of exile is reshaping the experience of forced displacement and its economic aspects. This includes the flipside of the digital economy's empowering promise: the formation of a globally dispersed crowd of digital exiles who lack the fundamental freedoms expressed by their stereotypical counterpart, the digital nomad. Exiles are commonly understood to be people who were forcibly displaced from their homeland. Unlike the term "refugee," which carries specific legal and humanitarian meaning, exile stems from ancient practices of banishment and forced displacement.[68] Displacement can lead to a prolonged condition of exile that is defined by ongoing forms of restriction that govern the lives and opportunities of displaced people in specific places and economies.[69] Thinking in terms of exile offers a critical perspective on the ongoing restrictions and risks refugees face as a result of their exclusion from, and unfavorable incorporation into, a digital economy.

The economic and virtual mobility a digital economy offers rarely turns refugees into digital nomads who have the freedom to move and work wherever they want. Consider, for a moment, refugees working remotely from camps who are only mobile in the sense that their work can travel beyond the boundaries of a refugee camp or host state, while their bodies are forced to stay put. Some manage to work and get paid remotely even as they cannot access employment locally. They may annotate images of street scenes in American cities to train AI models that power driverless cars, although they do not have the freedom to move to these very places. Remote refugee language tutors who are matched with language learners all over the world make new friends and learn about faraway places along the way. Yet, their lives remain firmly tethered to their local environment, be it a refugee camp in Kenya or a neighborhood of crisis-stricken Beirut. Against this backdrop, the concept of digital exile reminds us that the digital economy is not placeless or outside of people's local condition, even if the digital is often seen and framed "as being somewhere else."[70]

Emblematic of the failure of the digital economy to liberate many refugees from the restrictions and misery of exile was a conversation I had with Mahmoud, a Syrian remote Arabic tutor in Beirut who worked with the language learning enterprise NaTakallam. For US$10 an hour, he spoke Arabic with faraway clients who often became friends and whose lives and home countries he learned and cared about. "Language creates a direct connection between people. I see it as a first step to friendship. NaTakallam was like a window for me. I sit in my home, and it opens that window into a world," he said during our meeting in one of Beirut's cafés. When we talked about the discrimination against Syrians in Lebanon and the lack of suitable work opportunities, his eyes suddenly filled with tears. He told me he made plans to "cross the sea to Europe" soon. He was willing to risk his life to escape. Remote freelance work opened a window to the world for him, but he was unable to climb through it. He was grateful for the occasional online gig, but it was not enough to lift his spirits. He added, "Sometimes in online work, the worker will be like a slave. I say, 10 dollars in my situation per hour is great for me. But this fact at the same time also shows that this is not really respectful and decent work."

How can we make sense of the transnational digital mobility of work if refugee workers remain rooted in places of systematic marginalization and exclusion? How do we evaluate the seeming abundance of economic opportunity in the digital economy against the backdrop of refugees' exclusion from affordable connectivity and financial services, their restricted freedom to move and work, and their experiences of discrimination and degradation?

Looking at refugees in the digital economy as exiles reveals a new digitally mediated dimension of the "plurality of vision" that Edward Said ascribed to exiles, as people who are not only forcibly displaced from a homeland but also gain "an awareness of simultaneous dimensions" and frequently "cross borders, break barriers of thought and experience."[71] This plurality of vision now increasingly extends into a transnational digital economy that can augment the vision and economic world of refugees on the ground. With this augmentation comes a deepening rift: not only a rift between homeland and host country, but also the rift between a hypermobile digital economy they are invited to take part in and a disempowering condition of exile that continues to thrust them backwards.

By invoking the concept of digital exile, I acknowledge the exclusion and denial that affects refugees in the shadows of the digital liberation they are invited to embrace. The point is not that such exclusion outweighs the benefits of economic activity. The two become mutually constituent parts of the same experience: Refugees are susceptible to dreams of digital liberation and virtual mobility precisely because they are confined to camps and restricted by regulations and policies. Exile often involves a simultaneity of mobility and immobility, exclusion and inclusion, opportunity and its denial. At its heart lies a predicament of being in between worlds, balancing memories of a lost homeland and a stigmatized identity with the pressures to become someone new and to comply with conditions and rules set out by the host country or society. Crucially, exiles often feel "an urgent need to reconstitute their broken lives" and sometimes embrace "triumphant ideologies" in the process.[72] As I learned from highly motivated training course participants in Germany, Kenya, and Lebanon, digital jobs and online freelancing come to symbolize a new land of opportunity for refugees who want to reconstitute their socioeconomic lives. Their aspirations and hopes are fueled by an underlying "triumphant ideology" that digital jobs can liberate them from their condition. Unfortunately, the reality of being forcibly displaced and living in exile often undermines those aspirations, even if the possibility to earn money through digital means is real.

There are other reasons for invoking the ancient concept of exile. Refugees who seek to enter the space of a digital economy are confronted with forms of exclusion and marginalization not unlike those that exiles have often experienced upon arrival in a host country. Without the right documents and excluded by laws and regulations from national economies, their real human and economic potential is held at an unproductive tension between opportunity and its limitation. Just as they are invited to take part in the digital economy, its ostensibly universal offerings are only accessible to them under certain conditions that they struggle to meet: They must be digitally skilled, shift their mindset toward entrepreneurial thinking, accept unpaid labor time and underpaid work, invest what little they have left into expensive connectivity and devices, and embrace risk as a condition of opportunity. The promised land of digital opportunity is open to all those who can transform themselves through hard work and dedication. Yet so much of what holds refugees back lies beyond their control. Having the wrong kind of identity and status can be reason enough for someone to be cast out of the digital economy. As a result, many find themselves in a digital dimension of exile that harbors promising opportunities and simultaneously limits what refugees are entitled to. As people who are often already "rooted in the lost homeland, politically banished, immobilised and entrapped,"[73] digital exiles are banished and entrapped twice over.

Comparison Amid Diversity

Grounded in three very different national contexts—namely Lebanon, Kenya, and Germany—this book is as much a deep dive into each case study as it is a careful attempt at comparative analysis. The millions of Syrian refugees who have been hosted in European countries such as Germany rarely struggle to go online and most should not find it very difficult to buy a smartphone or a computer. Refugees in cities like Berlin have access to ample opportunities to develop digital skills and have a fair chance to find jobs in the tech-driven urban economy. Although in practice, barriers to developing their skills and finding employment abound, they have enjoyed the right to work and freedom of movement. This is a markedly different situation than that faced by refugees in crisis-affected Lebanon and by those living in Kenya. The Syrian refugees I met in Berlin's coding schools knew about online freelancing, but most of them did not really need it: Their chances to find decent work and formal employment in the local economy were real, even if ultimate success required a lot of effort and involved periods of unemployment or unpaid traineeships.

Different refugee populations also hold diverse capabilities and skills. Some Somali refugees in Kenya have carved out a niche as translators and online freelancers, while many Syrian remote freelancers have been teaching Arabic to students all over the world. Ukraine has supplied one of the largest global shares of workers on online freelance platforms, and a large part of its population has been subject to digital transformation and digital skills development before the war.[74] Even so, the majority of Ukrainians in Europe are unlikely to hold advanced and competitive digital skills even if they are well educated, as was the case among a cohort of

Ukrainian students at a coding course I visited in Vienna in 2024. While most of the participants had university degrees, including doctors, dentists, and art historians, most of them had no previous digital skill sets, and some did not own computers. They still hoped that developing their digital skills in software programming would ultimately be faster and more beneficial for their careers than trying to accredit and convert the degrees and qualifications they brought with them from Ukraine, a difficult process that can take several years and requires proficiency in the national language.

The need to account for this diversity demands a strong grounding of wider conclusions in specific case studies, complicating any broad-stroke statement about refugees in the digital economy. Understanding the opportunities and challenges a digital economy represents for refugees across these different cases nevertheless reveals striking similarities despite the differences: The promotion of digital skills and digital jobs as a solution for refugees has shaped a powerful imaginary of market-based liberation and freedom, with an implicit assumption that digital technologies have a capacity to bridge inequalities, leapfrog across geographic and socioeconomic barriers, accelerate integration and development processes, and circumvent limitations posed by discriminatory local labor markets. The digital economy therefore promotes a vision of digital hypermobility and economic inclusivity among refugees and the organizations that support them.

Although specific in their own ways, each of the case studies also exemplifies some regional dynamics: Syrian refugees in Western Europe lived in some of the world's richest economies and usually had the right to work and freedom of movement. Those who participated in coding schools in cities such as Berlin also found a strong demand for digitally skilled workers in the local economy. Refugees in Kenya who fled from countries such as Somalia and South Sudan predominantly lived in the confinement of camps but also witnessed a rapidly growing online gig economy while being able to tap into mobile money infrastructures that have eased digital payments in the region. Syrians in Lebanon suffered under the impact of economic crisis and violent conflict and faced a highly restrictive policy regime, as well as regulatory barriers to financial and digital inclusion that many economies in the Middle East shared.[75]

Overview of Chapters

The first of the three case study chapters launches the book's narrative from a highly challenging context that questions the feasibility of digital livelihoods to support refugees and other crisis-affected populations. We will see how Lebanon's multiple crises combine with Syrian refugees' digital and financial exclusion into an extremely challenging environment that undermines their capacity to benefit from a digital economy. It is precisely at a time of crisis that the need for digital and remote job opportunities reached its peak. Unfortunately, the very same crisis simultaneously eroded the foundations of an inclusive and functioning digital economy. This is in addition to a wide range of exclusionary regulations and policies that turn refugees into outcasts in a transnational digital economy, leading to a form of exile from the "planetary" space of a digital labor market.[76] In this sense, the digital economy becomes an extension of the exclusive dimensions of protracted exile instead of providing a remedy for its disempowering effects.

Moving from a context of severe restriction to a more enabling environment, chapter 2 then explores the ambivalent role of online freelancing among refugees in Kenya. It does so against the backdrop of the country's wider digital transformation and its refugee policies. Although remote freelance work provides a crucial job opportunity for some refugees who live in the confinement of camps, they also face a set of challenges and risks. A lack of recognized identification documents excludes many from digital tools and services, forcing them to innovate insecure workarounds that can entail risks and high costs. Other challenges include unreliable and time-restricted connectivity in refugee camps and the negative impact of precarious conditions in gig work. Rather than transcending the limitations of restrictive refugee spaces and policies, refugees' "adverse digital incorporation"[77] into the online gig economy in Kenya reveals how their vulnerabilities and risks are amplified and reinforced because of such digital economic inclusion. The digital economy in Kenya has ambivalent effects on refugees: It offers a seeming abundance of job opportunities and symbolizes a transnational space that can cross the borders of refugee camps at ease, and yet it also becomes a source of precarity and exposes them to a wide range of risks and harmful consequences.

Shifting the focus to a high-income country in Europe, chapter 3 shows how the journeys of refugee coding school students in the German city of Berlin are met by a high demand for skilled IT experts and an enabling economic environment. This instills powerful hopes for digital careers and employment among motivated training participants. As the learning of digital skills inspires ideas of a shortcut into formal employment, an ostensibly inclusive tech sector comes to symbolize a way around the barriers refugees face in entering more traditional sectors of the national economy. The realistic prospect of landing a decent job in the tech sector is supported by a wider enabling policy environment and rights, leading to a very low relevance of online freelancing and remote work as a potential alternative. At the same time, the pathways that lead from digital skills training toward employment are fraught with obstacles and challenging demands, such as the need to be a highly motivated and hardworking "good refugee" who accepts sacrifices and strives for recognition and integration against all odds.

The concluding fourth chapter first reflects on the continuously evolving nature of forced displacement and the digital economy while also taking stock of important developments since the research was conducted. A summary of chapter-specific insights is then followed by a wider comparative analysis that goes beyond each country level, offering a set of overarching key insights and outlining the wider implications and contributions of the research. Finally, an epilogue recenters the discussion around practical considerations about the current and future trajectory of digital refugee livelihoods, outlining a framework for an inclusive and fair digital refugee economy and discussing emerging trends and promising support models in theory and practice.

Methods and Research Background

This book is the culmination of around six years of research into the growing role a digital economy plays in the lives of forcibly displaced people. The research in Lebanon and Germany took place under a two-year project (2019–2021) that was funded by the Economic and Social Research Council UK. The interviews and on-site research were a combined effort between myself and the junior researchers who worked with me on the project—namely, Philip Rushworth and Watfa Najdi. After one month of initial fieldwork that I conducted in Lebanon in 2019, a second period of research in the country starting in March 2020 was cut short due to COVID-19 lockdown measures. Thereafter the impact of the pandemic shifted the research temporarily online, including to remote interviews and digital surveys.

The research in Berlin is based on forty-two interviews alongside many other informal conversations and observations during ethnographic fieldwork in 2019 and 2020, which focused primarily on coding schools and included participating in activities, such as career counseling sessions, workshops, and classes. In Lebanon, sixty-three semi-structured interviews were conducted with Syrian refugees and Lebanese citizens who took part in digital skills training programs or were active in digital and remote work. Another forty-three interviews were conducted with different experts such as staff at training programs, aid organizations, and the private sector. Additional data emerged from the participation in in-person and online events.

The data on Kenya is partly based on remote interviews I conducted during my work for the Employment, Labour Markets, and Youth branch of the ILO in 2021. Some of the insights also benefited from other ILO-funded research between 2022 and 2024. In very few cases, I used insights from interviews that were conducted by researchers I subcontracted at the social enterprise Samuel Hall. Other data from Kenya is based on focus group discussions involving some thirteen refugee participants held during a workshop in Nairobi in 2022. The workshop and focus groups, which also involved experts and practitioners alongside refugee participants, were co-organized and co-facilitated with my colleague Margie Cheesman and cohosted by John Warnes at UNHCR's Innovation Service with the support of UNHCR's country office in Nairobi.

The interviews and field research were complemented by five online surveys among the beneficiaries of several digital work and training initiatives in Lebanon and Germany, and globally. The surveys included both structured and open-ended questions and were distributed in collaboration with the relevant programs and enterprises. In Berlin, a collaboration with staff at the ReDI School in the design and distribution of a survey among their graduates reached 101 respondents. A survey targeting workers at two social impact platforms and enterprises in Lebanon that provided work in AI data training and image annotation yielded thirty responses from Lebanese and Syrian workers. Another survey designed and distributed in collaboration with the enterprise NaTakallam, through which refugee freelancers offered language services, reached 83 responses. The majority of respondents at NaTakallam were forcibly displaced people from a wider range of countries, and 43 percent were Syrians, with some fifteen of them having been based in Lebanon. A fifth survey with graduates of the Digital Skills Training program in Lebanon yielded thirty-one respondents, thirteen of which were Syrian and eighteen Lebanese.

The volume of data I have accumulated through several subsequent research engagements far exceeds the scope of this book. All of the research and applied work that I completed since 2017 somewhat shaped the body of knowledge that underpins the insights presented here. As expressed in more detail in the acknowledgments section, I am deeply grateful for the diverse collaborations this long-term work has involved.

All names of research participants from the refugee community have been fully anonymized with the use of pseudonyms. I have kept the real names of people only in some cases—for example, in the case of experts and officials who gave their permission to use their name.

1
Digital Exiles in Times of Crisis

The Struggle for a Digital Livelihood Among Syrian Refugees in Lebanon

Beirut was still alive and well during one of my early research visits to Lebanon, at least on the surface: Cafes and restaurants were busy with people whose salaries still held value, and the Lebanese lira traded for its officially fixed value of around 1,500 to the US dollar. This was before the country went into free fall to become one of the world's most severe economic crises since the mid-nineteenth century.[1] At the same time, Lebanon hosted the largest number of refugees per capita and per square kilometer in the world, with some 1.5 million Syrians living amid a total population of only 5.7 million. The government followed strict refugee policies that limited the Syrians' rights and their access to the labor market while also excluding them from banking services. Few could obtain official work permits, and the vast majority worked informally in sectors such as construction, agriculture, and cleaning services. Together with unreliable and expensive internet connectivity, all of this made Lebanon one of the most challenging grounds for connecting refugees to digital jobs and online income opportunities.

Another challenge lay in the educational profiles and digital skills capabilities of most Syrian refugees. As a digital communications expert named Joe told me during a meeting inside the Beirut compound of the UNHCR, "If we talk about first arrivals here, maybe 80 percent of them never used the internet. Ninety percent had never used ATM machines before." Only around three-quarters of Syrian heads of household in Lebanon went to primary school, and illiteracy was a widespread problem.[2] Although Joe noted a gradual behavior change among refugees from rural areas in adapting to cash machines and social media, he also emphasized that "to think about how digital technology can generate an income for refugees and work, I would think we are still far away from it."

Although this assessment dates back to 2017, many deeply rooted challenges continued to affect the feasibility of refugee work in a digital economy over the years that followed. Only a small minority of young and mostly well-educated Syrian refugees benefited from the digital sills training programs through which aid organizations, social enterprises, and educators aimed to equip them and Lebanese youth with marketable skills for a digital economy. One such training took place in a lecture room of the Lebanese International University in Beirut in July 2019, organized by the social enterprise Digital Opportunity Trust (DOT). Sitting in rows of fixed classroom benches, the small crowd of students attentively listened to their teacher Yasmeen, a young woman with a natural and sympathetic air of authority. The course she helped develop focused on *microwork*, which refers to the remote completion of basic information processing tasks, such as data entry, or image annotation and tagging, which are relatively automated, require minimal skills, and offer low renumeration paid per task.[3] This particular session focused on using the web content management system WordPress and its WooCommerce plug-in for digital work projects in the field of e-commerce.

"So, what are we doing here mainly?" asked Yasmeen, standing in front of the students waiting for a response. After a few seconds, one student broke the silence, saying, "It allows us to sell items online." Many of them hoped that their newly gained skills would soon allow them to make money as online freelance workers or digital entrepreneurs. What this could mean in practice became evident when they trialed a real-world digital work scenario: Provided with Excel sheets that listed the SKU numbers of clothing items, which is an identifier used to track stock, they had to find the matching images of each fashion piece online and enter them into a database. Some of the students later went on to work on similar projects with DOT's own social impact platform B.O.T., which stands for "Bridge, Outsource, Transform." As Yasmeen explained, such a work project might involve the following: "A company that maybe gets a new shipment of 15.000 items, they only have the data with the SKU numbers, but they don't want to hire a new staff member to set all this up. So, they outsource the work. They source it through B.O.T."

In the class filled with mostly young Lebanese students, Fadi, who was sitting in the row behind me, was the only Syrian. After taking previous trainings with DOT in basic digital literacy, social media, and mobile apps, he was now a university student in computer science and got a scholarship. Originally from the city of Idlib, he grew up without a father and was brought up by his single mother. He had studied electronics in Syria before the war displaced him to Lebanon. During the lunch break of the training course, we grabbed a cup of coffee from the vending machine in the hallway and walked down into the shaded courtyard of the tall concrete building.

Fadi was in many ways an exemplary candidate for the transformation digital livelihoods programs aspired to achieve: a highly motivated, skilled young refugee who aspired to succeed in a digital economy and invested into self-learning and skills development, even as the restrictions imposed on him undermined his chances. "I have been here for eight years, and I still can't get citizenship. I can't work in my field, in marketing. Online work is perfect because of that. I can work from home, from university, from every place," he said, thereby mirroring the idea that online work could bypass the restrictions refugees like him faced locally. "I want to work with [the social impact platform] B.O.T., in advertising maybe, marketing. It seems perfect, flexible time, flexible salary," he added. When I asked him if he already managed to earn money online, he shook his head, adding that he was trying. "The problem is, I can't get paid here. I don't have a Mastercard. I can't work from here and get paid."

Not only did national policies and practices prevent Syrians in Lebanon from opening bank accounts and getting debit or credit cards, they also increasingly excluded them from joining the workforce of key initiatives like B.O.T. This shattered the hopes of aspiring talents such as Fadi. Up until 2019, many initiatives trained and connected Syrian refugees to digital work opportunities, exploiting a legal gray area and a lack of government policies that explicitly restricted remote self-employed refugee work. Then, in July 2019, the Ministry of Labour issued a policy directive titled "Action Against Illegal Foreign Employment on the Lebanese Territory" that specifically targeted Syrians. The policy cited an "acute crisis in foreign employment" and "especially Syrian employment" that Lebanon suffered because "thousands of efficient and competent Syrian workers" were competing with Lebanese people in various sectors.

The policy took issue with what it saw as hundreds of thousands of Syrians working without permission in Lebanon. The ministry set out a plan in which they offered "violators" a one-month ultimatum to comply with the law while calling on employers to follow all other restrictions, such as those limiting certain jobs and professions to Lebanese workers. The policy fueled an already heated climate surrounding Syrian employment in Lebanon. A UN survey of the same year found that tensions between refugees and Lebanese host communities were on the rise, with over half of refugee families citing competition over jobs as a main source of such tension.[4] It was amid this challenging situation that digital skills training programs and new forms of digital work were being promoted to address the economic needs of Syrian refugees in Lebanon while also supporting vulnerable Lebanese citizens. Increasingly, however, the government became aware of these diverse initiatives and put pressure on aid organizations and enterprises to prioritize Lebanese citizens and refrain from supporting Syrians to find employment, effectively leading to their exclusion from the digital economy.

Against this backdrop, the case of digital livelihoods in Lebanon reveals the multilayered exclusion of refugees from the opportunities a digital economy can offer, despite the potentially transformative role it could play as a lifeline in times of crisis. Refugees who aspired to enter the digital economy were invited to nurture powerful ideas that digital jobs and online work can offer them lucrative income opportunities away from the restrictions they faced locally. Instead of being liberated in this sense, they experienced systematic forms of exclusion that marginalized them in a condition of digital exile. Those few refugees who managed to do paid remote work through enterprises and platforms experienced insecurity and precarity as part of such digital economic inclusion, even if it also offered them some benefits. The escalating impact of Lebanon's economic and financial crisis only further undermined their ability to benefit from a digital economy precisely at the time when they were in dire need of paid work for their economic survival.

While not covered within the time frame of this research, it is important to note that the economic crisis was soon followed by further devastation and instability: Israel's long-standing conflict with the Lebanese Shia group Hezbollah escalated in the aftermath of the October 7, 2023, attacks that the Palestinian Hamas carried out in Israel. In the wake of Israel's devastating military campaign in Gaza, Israeli bombardments and a ground invasion in Lebanon caused further devastation and displacement, including damages to digital infrastructures. These more recent devastations of war in the country were a painful reminder of its long history of instability and violence, including fifteen years of civil war (1975–1990) and almost two decades of Israeli occupation in the South (1982–2000), as well as recurring waves of conflict between Hezbollah and Israel.

Against the backdrop of recurring conflict and crisis, the absence of stability and continuing economic uncertainty have offered little respite for both Lebanese and Syrian refugees in the country. With the help of a diversity of pioneering initiatives and programs, Syrian and Lebanese youth in Lebanon nevertheless showed impressive resilience by continuing to struggle for economic opportunities and survival, sometimes innovating workarounds as they navigated the shifting landscape of a digital economy amid crisis and restriction.

Promoting Digital Livelihoods Amid Severe Restrictions

Promoting the digital economy as an alternative livelihood resource for Syrian refugees in Lebanon proved highly challenging. A range of digital skills training programs and social enterprises were active in the upskilling of Syrian refugees while experimenting with new solutions that could connect them to digital jobs. They associated the digital economy with a liberating quality that could virtually mobilize refugee workers beyond the restrictions at the national level. What many of these initiatives realized early on, however, was that the vast majority of refugees would need a lot of support to access the digital economy and its income-generating opportunities. This support included training courses ranging from digital literacy to software programming, help with internet access and equipment, and mentoring and career advice, as well as finding workarounds that allowed them to convert digitally earned money into cash.

The leading actors that developed and implemented such initiatives and programs included the DOT and its impact sourcing platform B.O.T., which were supported by the UN's International

Children's Emergency Fund (UNICEF); a social enterprise called Taqadam, which employed refugees to train data and models for the development of AI; the Digital Skills Training (DST) program at the American University of Beirut (AUB), which was funded by the World Food Programme (WFP) and piloted under its Innovation Accelerator, first under the name "Tech for Food" and later as "EMPACT"; and the social enterprise NaTakallam, which allowed refugees to sell remote language services such as conversational sessions. NaTakallam was initially launched in response to Syrian displacement in Lebanon but soon expanded globally to connect workers and clients in over 110 countries. The Bulgaria-based social enterprise Humans in the Loop, which sold AI data labeling services provided by refugees and workers in conflict-affected countries, also supported refugees in Lebanon with training and work opportunities.

Across these various initiatives, some fields of work emerged as more prominent and useful than others. One important market lay in the kind of language services that NaTakallam provided, connecting refugee tutors and conversation partners to paying language learners all over the world. The other important field was microwork and more specifically image labeling and image annotation, such as those microtasks and clicks that trained the AI behind driverless cars to independently recognize the difference between different objects, people, and situations. Digital labor platforms offered many kinds of jobs in online freelancing, many of which involve highly skilled work at higher levels of income.[5] The global demand on major online freelancing platforms was concentrated in more highly skilled fields such as software development and technology, creative and multimedia, writing and translation, and marketing and sales, although the lower skill category of "clerical and data entry" also made up a significant share of the global demand.[6] While digital livelihood initiatives aimed to connect refugees to jobs at both ends of the skill spectrum, highly skilled online and remote work often required advanced digital skills, proficiency in English, and other competencies that the average refugee lacked. These skill-related challenges intersected with many systematic barriers Syrians in Lebanon faced in accessing paid work on digital labor platforms, all of which effectively prevented them from realizing the potential of digital work to offer people a sustainable and secure source of employment in times of crisis.

Clamping Down on Digital Refugee Work

The nonstandard forms of work that digital platforms and enterprises enabled seemed like the perfect artifice in the shadow of the government's clampdown on informal Syrian workers. One could picture young Syrian men and women making money from their homes using computers or smartphones, without anyone knowing that they worked at all. As self-employed remote work among refugees was widely considered to be a legal gray zone in Lebanon, it offered a perceived sense of invisibility and flexibility in a policy context where formal employment was restricted. At first, aid organizations were thrilled and refugees were hopeful.

The romance between refugee aid and digital work did not last very long, however, as the government became increasingly aware of the initiatives and instructed the organizations that funded and ran these programs to stop including Syrian refugees. This included the UN's WFP, which funded the digital skills program that AUB developed and implemented successfully for many years. Despite being one of the largest UN aid organizations, WFP was unsuccessful in obtaining government endorsement of its program, effectively triggering Syrians' exclusion from some digital skills training courses, and especially from any direct promotion of digital employment.[7] What this meant for Syrian training participants like Fadi, whom we met earlier in the chapter, was that they would no longer be offered any paid work after completing their trainings, unlike the Lebanese students sitting in the same classrooms. As one manager of WFP's digital livelihoods program in Lebanon told me in July 2019, the organization could not continue to operate in a gray zone and potentially endanger its relationship with the Ministry of Social Affairs (MoSA), which implements WFP's National Poverty Targeting Programme that has supported Lebanon's poorest and most vulnerable families.

Perhaps understandably, the government wanted organizations to prioritize Lebanese citizens who faced rapidly rising levels of economic precarity, poverty, and unemployment. This opposition to connecting refugees to digitally mediated jobs was nevertheless a missed opportunity, as it ignored an important part of the argument for its significance: that refugees could make a livelihood online and remotely through digital platforms and sell their services to clients that are located elsewhere, without directly competing with the local Lebanese labor force. It could have been a win-win situation. The government stance was likely intended to make a case in point, although it felt unnecessary considering the small numbers of refugees who benefited from these initiatives. Moreover, most of the initiatives had already served Lebanese citizens alongside refugees across all of their programs anyway. Rabih Shibli, the director of the Center for Civic Engagement and Community Service at AUB, which ran the DST program, said in an interview, "The central government explicitly told the international agencies that they don't want such training programs anymore. I don't know the reason, and I can't speak on their behalf, but the reason is kind of obvious to me: They were afraid of them [the refugees] to become empowered and find jobs. Very bureaucratic and short sighted. This doesn't mean it can't happen. There are some organizations who can work without informing the ministry."

The impact sourcing platform B.O.T. had initially offered work to Syrian refugees alongside Lebanese youth. Syrians like Fadi, who built their skills in classrooms sitting next to Lebanese students, were originally allowed to earn money through digital work with B.O.T. after finishing their courses. According to the innovation specialist Tamara, who worked with UNICEF in Lebanon, B.O.T. had actually started with the idea to link refugees to digital work opportunities in 2016. Tamara knew Leila Janah, the social entrepreneur and founder of Samasource (who passed away in 2020). "I knew Leila and asked them to help us assess the playing field. They had expertise, and we wanted them to assess if it's a good idea," she explained. In October 2016, they assessed the situation, and UNICEF engaged in consultations with lawyers. "They said, up until now, there is a lot of gray areas and you can move forward with this. We didn't want to get into trouble with the government."

The project then piloted through the Lebanon branch of DOT in 2017. After an initial focus on training courses, the platform B.O.T. was created to ensure that trainees also gained access to concrete job opportunities after they completed the course. But when the government issued its circular against informal Syrian employment in 2019, B.O.T. was forced to stop offering work to Syrian refugees after they completed their training courses. "B.O.T. is bound by regulations that prohibit the employment of any non-Lebanese student," said Marianne, the country director of the DOT and managing director of B.O.T. She added that "in the current situation, we cannot take an invoice from or pay a Syrian refugee."

Economic Exclusion and Rising Humanitarian Needs

Their exclusion from the newly promoted digital work opportunities came at a difficult time for Syrian refugees, who suffered under an increasingly dire economic and humanitarian situation. At the time of the government's policy against informal Syrian work in 2019, some 57 percent of Syrian refugee families lived in overcrowded shelters and homes. Although the country's economy was not yet in free fall, Syrian refugees faced rising levels of food insecurity, economic vulnerability, and household debt.[8] Some 66 percent of men and only 11 percent of Syrian refugee women participated in the labor force at the time, amid an overall unemployment rate of 31 percent, which was far higher in the major refugee-hosting regions of Bekaa (62 percent) and Baalbek-El Hermel (49 percent). The dominant sectors in which refugees worked were construction, agriculture, and services, while large sectors of the labor market remained inaccessible to them. This difficult situation forced many to adapt by reducing food consumption and the number of meals per day.[9]

The majority of forcibly displaced Syrians in Lebanon, who were not recognized as "refugees" by the government, were officially required to obtain a work permit, although the vast majority had little choice but to work informally. This included brokered work in agriculture and factories without employee contracts and protection.[10] In agriculture and construction, the sectors in which the greatest number of Syrian refugees worked, employers did not contribute to social security, and workers remained excluded from the labor law.[11] Syrian refugees who aimed to work in sectors other than those explicitly allowed faced a wide range of obstacles to obtain work permits, including high fees, frequent rejection, and discrimination based on the principle that Lebanese nationals are to be given priority or that certain quotas of nationals must be met. A large number of sectors and professions remained limited to Lebanese nationals,[12] including some professions that are relevant for the digital economy, such as "computer officer," "e-business," or "engineer."[13]

Syrian refugees in Lebanon who wanted to open a business would officially need to follow the same procedures as all other foreigners, including minimum required capital, a national ID or passport, and a work permit.[14] Online self-employment and freelance work would normally be governed by business regulations, but there was no clarity about what regulations and laws might apply for refugee workers and sole traders. This regulatory vacuum helped keep the idea alive that online and remote work may continue to offer refugees a way to circumvent a restrictive national labor market despite the government's opposition. After all, online freelance work has been promoted in several other restrictive contexts for its ability to bypass barriers and local laws.[15]

Refugees' developed strong hopes that online freelancing and remote work may help them to escape the restrictive policies and laws that defined their lives in exile. These hopes also resulted from their recurring experiences of exclusion and discrimination: Some 62 percent of Syrian graduates surveyed at the DST program stated "because I am Syrian" in response to a question about the major barrier they faced in finding a job in Lebanon. As the Syrian digital skills training participant Maher said in an interview, "As a Syrian, if I want to look for work or apply for job opportunities, the first thing that the employer will ask for is my papers, my residency, and I do not have one. There are also priorities. Employers would hire a Lebanese applicant for any vacancy before they consider a Syrian applicant. Also, they will always choose someone who has a university degree or has more experience. I have neither."

Many joined digital skills training programs hoping that they would lead to jobs that do not require papers and do not expose them to discrimination. The informality and lack of regulation in the digital economy further deepened the insecurity and risks many already faced in local informal jobs, while promoting a kind of worker invisibility that has been a long-standing feature of platform work.[16] My friend Ara, who used to work as a teacher and studied chemistry in Syria before being displaced to Lebanon, started freelancing remotely in 2019 for a company in Canada and another in Indonesia. Although he said that lawyers had told him online freelance work was not explicitly illegal for Syrians in Lebanon, he kept this work invisible as far as possible, saying, "On my LinkedIn, I don't mention these jobs for my own protection." The informality and invisibility of online work was seen as a way around local restrictions and control but also became a source of insecurity and precarity.

Precarious Digital Work as a Means of Survival

Sitting in a café in the densely populated Beirut district of Bourj Hamoud, I met the seventeen-year-old Syrian Hiba and her twenty-one-year-old brother Khaled. Both of them worked on a freelance basis with a US-based social enterprise called Taqadam, which generated an income for refugees in Lebanon through work in image annotation and visual data training for AI. After we ordered our drinks and got to know each other a little better, Hiba took a laptop out of her bag and opened it for a quick demonstration of the work they currently did. With a few clicks, she opened an annotation tool that showed a satellite image of buildings surrounded by fields. "There is the name of the company, the address, we go to Google Maps and look for the name of the company. These are chemical companies," she said, adding, "We are measuring the size of the company . . . annotating if it is a sale location, a warehouse. . . . The knowledge comes with experience and training."

As Hiba marked the boundaries of buildings in the image, she explained that she had worked on many similar projects before. She enjoyed the work even if she didn't really know what the ultimate purpose of the project was or who had contracted the work. I asked if she worked on other projects at the moment. She nodded and opened the mobile version of the annotation tool on her smartphone. This project was about driverless cars, her brother Khaled explained. Hiba showed a photograph of an urban street scene and pointed at different objects, labeling items such as a "pedestrian" and a "car." This kind of work is an example of the human-powered tasks that train the AI behind automated cars, thereby improving its vision and classification of objects and people in images. "Is this

San Francisco?" I asked her, wondering whether I guessed the location of the photograph right. "I don't know. I never know where it is," she answered. "I just tag the images."

For Hiba and Khaled, their five siblings, and their parents, such digital work had quickly become an important contribution to their household income. This livelihood resource hung precariously on a fine string for as long as the entire family only had one laptop, which Hiba shared with her brother. Their younger sixteen-year-old sister was also working occasionally, and sometimes even the younger siblings, aged ten and nine, contributed with a few playful clicks. Turning their digital work into a family business allowed them to deliver projects faster and to share the available times between them. With the money they made over the first year, they could finally afford a second laptop. The work was often hard and tiring though. Hiba said she usually worked all day when she was on a project, also being responsible for checking the quality of other workers' annotations. Khaled, who worked as an assistant in a tailor shop during the day, said, "I get home and eat dinner, then I sit a bit with family, and then I open the laptop to work for three or four hours. This gives me some income." How much money they earned was difficult to estimate since payments were calculated by the number of annotations they did, and different projects added up to different hourly, daily, or monthly pay. "Let's say for two hours, we make six dollars," said Khaled, offering a rough estimate.

In an online survey among twenty-six Lebanese and four Syrians who worked as image annotators with Taqadam and the impact sourcing platform B.O.T., the average monthly income that respondents estimated was US$270 at an average 35 hours of work per week. By international and also national standards, this was a low level of pay even at this time before the financial crisis, when the exchange rate to the Lebanese pound was still fixed. In practice, something like an "average" week did not really exist for self-employed digital workers because they could be without projects and income for weeks or even months. They also did not have insurance and had no access to employment benefits, sick leave, or other rights and entitlements associated with formal employees. As Charbel, the business development and marketing director at B.O.T., explained the arrangement in 2022,

> They are freelancers. They work with us on a freelance project-based term. What we provide them with is cost either per day or per productivity level. So, let's say today they're working on data collection. What we can do is either pay them based on the data collected, successful data entered, or per day. First, we assess how much work they can do in a day; for example, they can do up to like twenty data rows, and we probably pay them per successful completion of that. As for direct benefits, such as insurance plans, etc.—no, they are not available at the moment.

Evaluating the working conditions among the beneficiaries of social impact enterprises that supported refugees and other marginalized populations is not as straightforward as it seems. They do not usually provide insurance or employment benefits, classifying potentially vulnerable refugee workers as self-employed contractors in ways similar to how major digital labor platforms approached them. Such digital work takes place under precarious conditions that are hardly ideal for forcibly displaced people who are already in economically vulnerable positions. At the same time, social impact platforms and enterprises provide skills training and other vital support to workers while also doing their best to convince clients to price projects in a way that results in an acceptable pay per worker. Despite the underlying precarity, for the Syrian refugees who managed to do such paid work fairly regularly, it often became a vital resource to complement their livelihoods in a highly restrictive context.

A persistent problem was that training programs only led to a job and a regular income for very few among the participating refugees. This created a tension between their experienced reality and the enthusiastic promotion of these approaches, leading to unrealistic hopes. Additional disappointment resulted from the failed experiments and innovations within programs that ultimately did not convert their learning into earning opportunities.

Dampened Hopes and Failed Experiments

Hiba and her brother initially had high expectations when they first started developing their digital skills through training courses. The opportunity to work with Taqadam only came up by chance after a year-long job search had almost left them without hope, despite having participated in the DST program at AUB in 2017. The course had offered them six months of training in core programs such as Microsoft Excel, alongside specific training on image annotation. Khaled said, "We joined it in the hope to find work afterwards. They promoted it in the way that you can use it to work online afterwards." In reality, he lamented, they were only involved in what he called a "short piece of work" that was "badly paid." After that, they "sat back at home without any work."

In a similar vein, the Syrian training participant Bilal joined his first digital skills training after having lost his job, saying, "I was very excited to sign up because I wanted to make a shift in my life and start my own work. . . . I felt like my life is about to change, like I have been offered a great chance to shift my life around and succeed. I felt like I finally found what I have been looking for." In the end, he was "devastated," as he put it. "After the trainings, I learned more skills, but what I learned and what I know now is not enough. Any child nowadays, with a laptop at home, knows as much as I know." The difficulty to develop competitive skills that enable refugees to compete for jobs independently meant that digital work with a lower barrier to entry, such as the image annotation Hiba and Khaled did, was often the most feasible option. Many others felt that they would need much more support to find work independently, some even being unaware what online freelancing was or how they could ever access it as refugees in Lebanon.

Samir, a twenty-nine-year-old Syrian who studied psychology and took part in several cycles of digital skills training since 2018, said in March 2021 that his main reason for joining was "that I did not know how to use a computer at all. . . . I started from zero." He lamented that the three-month training courses were simply not enough to learn computer programming for someone like him. When asked if he considered freelancing on some of the major global platforms as a way out of his joblessness, he said, "I do not know what online freelancing is. . . . Even if I knew about it, I do not have the adequate skills to pursue this type of work." The need for English language skills posed another barrier. According to Samir, this "is the biggest obstacle anyone could face, as all programming languages require knowledge of English. Otherwise, you would not be able to improve your skills. This limits my chances a lot."

The WFP-funded DST program Hiba and her brother took part in first launched as a pilot with some one hundred students in 2016. By 2019, it had around 1,300 Syrian and Lebanese participants per year who took courses ranging from basic computer literacy to more advanced levels in web design and programming. Courses were offered across several digital training centers in Lebanon. In many ways, the program was a great success. However, the challenges of Lebanon's crumbling economy and government restrictions imposed on refugees' vocational training and employment undermined the program's ability to turn learning into earning. Tapping into a global digital economy by facilitating online and platform work was one of the original aims of the initiative, but only very few refugees managed to find a job afterward. Some of them had their high hopes shattered by a failed humanitarian experiment. Such experimental humanitarianism often tests unproven approaches and technologies in crises and emergencies, using vulnerable people who are in need of aid as the testing ground to develop new projects and programs through pilots.[17]

One aim of the program's early pilot was to facilitate real work opportunities. At one point, this aim was meant to be realized through a collaboration with the AI company Figure Eight (later acquired by Appen), which had previously provided remote work opportunities for refugees and people affected by disasters elsewhere. As Sarah, who comanaged the DST program at AUB, explained to me during a meeting in July 2019, "We had a group of graduates in March. We wanted to connect them to the Figure Eight platform. . . . The problem was, and this refers to a lot of platforms, that Lebanon was a blacklisted country. So, the platform had to white-list the participants individually."

This attempted solution to selectively enable each participant to access the platform despite Lebanon being a blacklisted location failed. As the computer scientist Haidar, who worked with DST on the project, told me in a meeting at AUB's campus in Beirut, "The platform did not allow IP addresses from Lebanon to access the platform. They said they might be able to wait, allocated individual IP addresses; but IP addresses here are dynamic, the service providers keep changing IP addresses. . . . . This was tiring and it did not work." His colleague Wassim, who also helped develop the DST program, added, "This was our major hope to get people to make some money. We taught students that knew nothing, and they graduated knowing lots of things. The problem is that only a very small number got jobs. Once we had a very good platform for them to make money, logistically, it didn't work."

In addition to these technical barriers, the program was affected by a pause in external funding that resulted in the temporary suspension of training courses, leaving many participants without the continuous support and opportunities they had hoped for. The Syrian woman Marwa, who took part in two cycles of DST training courses in the city of Sidon, was one of those affected. She lamented that the courses did not provide enough specialized skills to find a job, and the interruption made things worse. Speaking during a remote interview from Damascus, where she stayed temporarily for medical treatment, she said, "You are telling me a story, but not the end of it. When we were faced with the labor market, we saw how much we were lacking."

She found this sobering reality especially disappointing because she strongly believed that working as an online freelance web designer was the perfect job for her, personally and as a woman living in a particular sociocultural context: "Now, web design is the best job for females in the Middle East because we can work from the house. This is the most important factor for women in the Middle East. I have to work from the house because it is forbidden to work outside a lot, to go to work and come back late. . . . Working online from home would be very good. We would have work, a source of money, while still being able to stay at home with children. We won't come back late from work." Home-based digital work through platforms and enterprises was also a desirable option for Hiba, who said that it was especially suitable for her "as a woman." She added that the only other work she could find were cleaning jobs in private houses, which she and her family did not consider appropriate.

Refugee women in the Middle East and North Africa region have faced logistical and social barriers that make them less likely to work than their male counterparts, including the inability to undertake long and precarious commutes while balancing family duties. "Some are also faced with constant pressures from their families or community, including scrutiny and judgement over the long hours or other commitments involved in undertaking a job."[18] This has turned home-based remote work into a powerful aspiration. Unfortunately, a more sobering reality of being excluded from the benefits of a digital economy often dampened these hopes. A survey among 542 Syrian and Lebanese DST participants in 2019, who had participated in trainings during the preceding twelve months, showed that only 13 percent of the graduates were working.[19] As the digital skills training graduate Rashid said, "What I hoped for is that . . . we would be connected to opportunities, or those who had high grades and graduated on the top of their class would be provided with jobs. But that did not happen. We learned the skills perfectly, but then we were left on our own." However, even if these graduates of training programs would have developed highly competitive digital skills for successful work on global digital platforms, they would have still faced digital and financial exclusion at multiple levels.

The Digital and Financial Exclusion of Syrian Refugees in Lebanon

Many factors that undermined the outcomes of digital skills training programs in Lebanon were beyond the involved actors' sphere of influence. These factors included not only the government's restriction of Syrians' access to employment and digital work opportunities but also the refugees' systematic financial and digital exclusion: They faced barriers to connectivity and often could not afford digital devices, they were excluded from the financial services that are needed to work and sell services online, and they were prevented from joining and using major digital platforms. Although many initiatives responded to this exclusion with ad hoc innovations and workarounds, it fundamentally undermined the capacity of the digital economy to liberate refugees from the restrictions and economic deprivation they faced as protracted exiles in Lebanon.

Exclusion from Meaningful Connectivity

Unreliable and slow internet affected all of Lebanon but especially rural areas and districts that hosted large numbers of refugees.[20]

Frequent electricity outages posed a fundamental challenge for digital and remote workers because it disrupted their workflows and could lead to delayed submission of their work at given deadlines, which might result in negative reviews or financial losses. The private generators that households used to fill gaps in electricity provision incurred additional costs and were often unreliable. The economic crisis further slowed the rollout of fiber-optic cables and 5G services,[21] although fixed broadband was largely nonexistent in refugee households anyway. Mobile phones were the primary means to access the internet, as the vast majority of Syrian refugee households in Lebanon had a mobile phone, and some 85 percent had access to a smartphone.[22] However, in some areas such as Tripoli (North) and Akkar, a rural area, Lebanese households were almost twice as likely to own a smartphone than Syrian refugees.[23] The need for a personal computer further complicated access to the digital economy for many graduates of digital skills training programs, who often owned no computers at all, or they had to share devices with other family members and take turns using them.

Effectively using a smartphone for data-intensive digital work posed another problem because internet connectivity has become highly expensive in Lebanon. In 2023, the cheapest mobile broadband plan providing at least 2 GB per month cost 10 percent of per capita income, compared to the world average of 1.25 percent.[24] Changes in the exchange rate that was used to fix mobile tariffs had led to a fivefold increase for a prepaid card at one point,[25] turning Lebanon into one of the most expensive countries for mobile internet.[26] All of this excluded refugees from *meaningful connectivity*, which would entail a safe, productive, and affordable online experience.[27] The lack of affordability undermined refugees' chances to make an income from digital and remote work while also decreasing their ability to advance their skills through e-learning independently. Combined with their frequent hope in the future returns from the investments they made, the cost of connectivity put refugees at financial risks if these returns never really materialized. Their simultaneous exclusion from the bank accounts and financial services that are needed to get paid for digital and remote work further derailed their digital livelihood journeys.

Exclusion from Financial Services

Although Syrian refugees faced specific barriers, their financial exclusion was embedded in the wider challenges online freelancers and remote workers faced at the national level. These become clear in a thread on the community platform Reddit: Here, a user introduces himself as a Lebanese-Canadian software engineer and writes about online freelancing on platforms such as Fiverr and Upwork, offering his advice for other people in Lebanon who would like to make an income online. Those replying to his well-intended post point out that the Israeli platform Fiverr is banned in Lebanon, while PayPal is not available, just as one of the few digital alternatives for payments, the e-wallet Payoneer, is blocked. Another user writes that "we can't use credit cards [at the moment], and the transactions require USD which is nonexistent at this point," with another adding that "all these websites and payment methods are banned in Lebanon."

These wider limitations affected Syrian refugees who wanted to work online and remotely disproportionally, because regulations and exclusive practices prevented them from opening accounts with conventional banks and financial services. Some 78 percent of Syrian graduates surveyed at the DST program listed a lack of access to bank accounts and bank cards as a major barrier to online work, compared to 31 percent among Lebanese graduates. Among the fifteen Lebanon-based workers surveyed at the language learning enterprise NaTakallam, six out of the seven Syrians stated that not having access to bank accounts is a major barrier to working online, which was not the case among the Lebanese respondents, although

86 percent across both groups stated that they faced "difficulties getting paid from online work."

The main reasons behind these barriers are regulations and policies. Like many other countries, Lebanon followed Know Your Customer (KYC) and Customer Due Diligence requirements, which require proof of identity and often additional documentation for individuals to conduct financial transactions and open a bank account, such as proof of address and residency permits. Syrian refugees in Lebanon could not usually meet these ID requirements.[28] As early as 2011, at the outset of the war in Syria, the Association of Lebanese Banks instructed all banks to limit their relations with Syrian clients and prohibit transactions in US dollars for Syrian-held accounts—measures that were directly linked to sanctions that prohibit "all transactions or dealings" with any person subject to US sanctions on Syria.[29] The resulting lack of account ownership often imposed a full stop on the hopeful digital livelihood journeys of refugees who graduated from training courses, who were incentivized to consider working online and remotely but were simultaneously unable to get paid for any work they may have found.

As the Syrian training graduate Raed said, when he was asked if he had considered working as an online freelancer, "They told us about this [online freelancing] during the trainings. But they said that we need a bank account to start working. There is no way I can get a bank account, so I did not try it or look up opportunities even. Why would I do that, if at the end I will hit a wall if I do not have a bank account? I would work and work and then for nothing. . . . If I had a bank account, I would have been more encouraged to pursue this."

Unable to make use of formal channels in their own name, some tried to find informal workarounds like channeling payments through the accounts of family members and friends. However, this was not usually an acceptable means of payment by employers or platforms. In other refugee contexts, such as Kenya, exclusive KYC regulations and ID requirements have similarly pressured refugees into informal and risky workarounds, such as using proxy bank accounts, SIM cards, and mobile money wallets registered under someone else's identity.[30] Yet even if they found a way to get paid for online and remote work, Syrian refugees in Lebanon often also faced blanket exclusion from the digital platforms that offered such work, both because they were Syrian and because they were in Lebanon.

Exclusion from Digital Platforms

Syrian refugees in Lebanon faced specific restrictions in accessing digital labor platforms that were linked to their location and their nationality, mostly because of the same KYC requirements and international sanctions that limited their access to financial services. Most major digital labor platforms require a government-issued ID and frequently demand additional proof of address and other documentation. Some nationalities, including Syrians, were categorically excluded from joining platforms, which often stipulate that they "do not permit registration of people from countries that are subject to sanctions."[31] This phenomenon is by no means limited to Syrians in Lebanon. Forcibly displaced people in Sudan, for example, were equally affected by sanctions and continue to face a long list of restricted digital technologies, while their refugee ID cards do not meet the requirements of SIM card registration or KYC requirements of financial services.[32]

The barriers to joining digital labor platforms for Syrians are well illustrated by an online post in an Upwork forum by a user called Hussein: "Hello, I'm a Syrian but I live in Lebanon, currently I'm trying to verify my account and I have 2 issues: Syria is not listed in the dropdown menu when I try to select the ID issue country. There is only one accepted, the passport, but I don't have that I have a birth certificate paper, I can't get the passport because of the war there. I hope you consider my situation, thank you."[33]

Many other users responded to the same thread over the years. In 2023, one posted, "im having the same problem can you help me please. im syrian and i live in Egypt," and another user wrote, "Hello, can anyone from the support team create a support ticket for me as well? I have the same issue here, Syrian residing in Turkey." The categorical exclusion of Syrians from some of the most important online freelancing platforms, alongside their financial exclusion and other barriers they faced nationally, combine to relegate them into a digital space of restriction and marginality that mirrors in many ways their wider condition of being forcibly displaced in Lebanon: a space of digital exile at the extreme margins of a planetary digital economy.[34] The rapid emergence of Lebanon's economic crisis only further cemented this marginality for Syrian refugees and many of the Lebanese host community members.

Digital Livelihoods Under the Impact of Economic Crisis

Much has happened in Lebanon since the first digital livelihoods initiatives emerged there in 2016. The official clampdown on informal refugee work in 2019 and the subsequent exclusion of Syrians from training programs and digital work initiatives were a serious obstacle to these pioneering efforts. The impact of the large-scale economic and financial crisis that followed further undermined the feasibility of connecting refugees to digital jobs and remote work. Aid-funded initiatives continued to promote online freelancing and digital skills training as a potential form of humanitarian relief for crisis-affected people, even if the participation of Syrian refugees had become increasingly unfeasible.

The crisis further deepened economic vulnerabilities among both Syrian refugees and Lebanese citizens. Poverty levels more than tripled in a single decade to encompass 44 percent of the total population,[35] some 56 percent of the total working age population were outside the labor force, and 62 percent of all employment was informal—a rate that rose to 95 percent among vulnerable Syrian refugees.[36] Lebanon further experienced one of the highest rates of food price inflation in the world, which exacerbated the precarity of living conditions for the poorest and most vulnerable segments of the population.[37] As the local economy crumbled and unemployment soared, large numbers of Lebanese emigrated, but some of the highly skilled talents who remained in the country increasingly looked to online freelance work as an alternative.

"I Will Survive": Searching for a Digital Lifeline in Crisis

An emerging economic crisis fueled new international campaigns that appealed to the large Lebanese diaspora to outsource jobs remotely for people in Lebanon. The most vocal of these initiatives, Jobs for Lebanon, "started with the revolution in Lebanon in October, when people were really excited for change," said Roy, an entrepreneur who cofounded Jobs for Lebanon and its global umbrella, Jobs for Humanity, in March 2020. He got a phone call from a friend who was a venture capitalist in London, who had just returned from leave and found twelve messages from Lebanese people asking him for a job. "The solution and idea was to have a global campaign to call upon the diaspora, the Lebanese expats, to hire Lebanese on a freelance basis." They created the Jobs for Lebanon platform, which aimed to match local applicants with job postings from the diaspora to support the population in times of crisis. While its emphasis was on creating jobs for Lebanon and the Lebanese, Baladi underlined in our conversation that Syrian refugees were not excluded from the initiative.

The belief that remote work and a transnational digital economy could bring economic relief to crisis-affected Lebanon was set against a backdrop of a rapidly growing platform economy.[38] Lebanon's share of the total global freelance workforce on major platforms, as measured by the Online Labour Index, was at 0.7 percent between 2017 and 2018, which is not insignificant for the small country—but this share collapsed to a mere 0.07 by 2023.[39] This sharp drop, which may have been impacted by a disabling economic crisis and resulting difficulties to receive international payments, points at a paradoxical situation: that online and remote work became increasingly unfeasible for people in Lebanon precisely when they needed it most. This was especially true for Syrian refugees who were disproportionally affected by barriers to digital inclusion and digital work. Their reality stood in sharp contrast to the promotion of e-commerce and online work as a liberating and boundary-crossing alternative that is easy to access.

Amid a deepening economic crisis in Lebanon, the initiative "I Will Survive" launched a virtual event to support young people to make money online. Speakers presented e-commerce and online freelancing as "easy tools" that would allow participants to "start making money tonight." One speaker, a successful online freelancer based in the Gaza Strip, Palestine, said that "all you need to become a successful freelancer is a technical skill, motivation, English skills, a laptop, an email, fast internet connection, and a credit card." This optimism was soon met by questions from participants that reflected a different reality, such as those asking how they can make money online without a bank account and with payment services like PayPal being unavailable in Lebanon. Then the online event was disrupted by one of the many electricity outages that were a daily occurrence at the time, disconnecting most attendees from the internet and adding further doubt about their ability to access the ostensibly boundless digital opportunities at a time of economic crisis and infrastructural collapse.

The Erosion of Digital Infrastructures

The crisis gradually worsened the reliability of internet connectivity and made it even less affordable. The digital economy lost the necessary foundations to function as ICT infrastructures eroded and digitalization efforts came to a halt. An update to Lebanon's digital transformation strategy in 2022 acknowledged the collapse of infrastructure and the shrinking of technological capabilities.[40] Fuel shortages disrupted internet connectivity, and the country came close to an internet blackout in March 2023 during persistent strikes by employees of the state-run telecom company Ogero.[41] These disruptions and rising connectivity costs affected refugees disproportionally, as they are among the most economically vulnerable and often live in areas with low internet connectivity and a lack of fixed internet infrastructure.

Both Syrian and Lebanese interviewees spoke of how increasingly unreliable connectivity undermined their ability to make a digital livelihood, posing financial and reputational risks if their work could not be completed at deadlines. Nadia, a Syrian digital skills training graduate, said, "I used to scream and curse all the time. I fought every day with my internet provider. I had deadlines and submission dates, and the internet would just cut off. It drove me crazy. When that happened, I had to work at night to make up for the lost hours." Sara, a Lebanese woman working with the impact sourcing platform B.O.T., said, "During the time I was working with B.O.T., the internet connection was fine, but the problem was the power cuts. Even the private generator turns off because it cannot provide electricity for that long. So, there are like four hours per day, sometimes more, where we do not have any electricity or internet. During this time, I could not work." Adding to connectivity problems was that currency devaluation and inflation made imported electronic goods highly expensive, further affecting the affordability of internet connectivity and digital devices discussed earlier. One freelancer, Reem, a Lebanese graduate of the coding school Codi, said, "My laptop is very old, and it is very challenging for me to use it, especially that I take on different projects at the same time. However, buying a new one is not an option right now because of the economic crisis. I just have to work with it."

As the government acknowledged the collapse of digital infrastructures and connectivity barriers, it also cited a lack of digital skills and "outdated laws and regulations" while stating that "closing the digital divide starts with increasing physical access through ICT infrastructure" and advocating for "universal access" and a "whole-of-society" approach.[42] The strategy did not mention refugees as an important part of this challenge, despite Lebanon being the highest per-capita refugee-hosting country in the world. Many refugees were ill equipped to prepare themselves for a digital world of work, and the economic crisis further undermined their capacity to benefit from digitalization.

Growing Difficulties in Developing Skills

The combined impact of forced displacement and an economic crisis undermined the capacity of Syrians in Lebanon to develop the skills they needed for a digital economy. Those without higher education were less likely to have the skills and knowledge required to benefit from online freelancing opportunities. By one measure, some 60 percent of workers on remote work platforms are highly educated with university degrees, which rises to 73 percent among workers in developing countries.[43] Digital livelihood initiatives in the development and humanitarian sectors often prioritized beneficiaries who already had a certain level of digital literacy and skills, even if they also tried to advance the digital literacy of those who started from scratch. University students were a main target group in Lebanon, partly because they were more likely to demonstrate a positive impact of training programs since their starting point was more advanced than that of others without similar education.

For example, some 77 percent of the workers surveyed at the data annotation enterprise Taqadam had a graduate university degree, while the remaining 23 percent all had an undergraduate degree or currently studied toward one. At the language teaching enterprise NaTakallam, which also had some fifteen freelancers based in Lebanon, 53 percent of their global workforce had a bachelor's degree, and another 19 percent had a graduate degree. Women and men from marginalized backgrounds with low educational levels were specifically encouraged to join digital literacy and skills trainings, but they were not always the ones who succeeded in the highly competitive digital marketplaces.

The impact of forced displacement and an economic crisis on refugees' education in Lebanon put them at a disadvantage. As many households lost their income during the crisis, they lost their ability to send their children to schools.[44] Fewer students entered universities, and many dropped out because the devaluation of the Lebanese currency reduced their capacity to pay.[45] Only very few Syrian refugees could access higher education or even continue primary and secondary school in Lebanon.[46]

Riham, a Syrian refugee who came to Lebanon with her family in 2013, could not enroll at a university until 2016, saying that she lost three years of her education. By 2020, in the midst of the COVID-19 crisis, she studied but could not register for some courses, explaining that "it depends if we have enough money that semester or not." Apart from one short project with an outsourcing platform, she never found work despite having done several cycles of digital skills training and regularly screening Whatsapp groups for freelancing opportunities. Another Syrian refugee, Rashid, said that when he came to Lebanon, he could not enroll at a university because "the process needs a lot of papers and documents, as well as a valid legal residency, which I do not have. . . . It also costs a lot of money."

"Impossible to Get Paid": Restrictions to Financial Services

Accessing stable foreign currency such as US dollars from a country that is affected by currency devaluation and an economic crisis could be one of the key benefits of remote and online work. In Venezuela, for example, digital platforms have offered to some workers the right resources, skills, and capital to withstand economic disruption, but this survival strategy was undermined by sanctions and regulations similar to those affecting payments and access to platforms in Lebanon.[47] The potential of online and remote work as a relief strategy in crisis nevertheless continued to inspire hopes for a possible way out. Ziad, a Lebanese worker with the platform B.O.T., said in August 2020 that the lack of local job opportunities under the impact of overlapping crises made him "look for opportunities abroad." However, from late 2019 onward, Lebanese banks had locked depositors out of their dollar accounts and blocked transfers abroad. Later, banks imposed varying limits on the number of dollars any depositor can withdraw.[48] These measures undermined the capacity of transnational digital labor markets to transcend the specific constraints of the local economy.

Reem, a Palestinian Lebanese graduate of a coding school who worked as a freelancer for companies in the UK, said in November 2020, "When the financial crisis started, our salaries got stuck in the bank because of the restrictions on dollar withdrawal." However, she added that she managed to open a "fresh" US dollar account with another bank to receive her income from freelance work, although she lost all her savings that were locked into the previous account. "I am the only one working in my family now. So, I am the main provider. I am managing well because I get paid in US dollars, but sometimes it gets really stressful."

Bank accounts in US dollars that existed prior to emergence of the crisis in 2019 were initially inaccessible and have been subjected to withdrawal limits and conversion rates below the market rate, while those opened afterward were commonly referred to as "fresh dollar" accounts and did not have these limitations. The Lebanese digital skills training graduate Omar found that his long-standing problem to get paid for online freelancing worsened under the crisis, to the point that "it is impossible to get paid." He and other remote workers had to find informal workarounds, such as using other people's bank accounts or storing money in an e-wallet, if they managed to open one at all. While Lebanese citizens usually managed to open fresh dollar accounts, this was rarely possible for Syrian refugees.

As the impact of the crisis worsened, the experienced programmer Ara from Syria lamented that his workaround of getting paid through a cousin's account was no longer acceptable to his client. Unable to open a USD account, he was left with the only option of Western Union cash transfers that incurred a sizeable fee and unfavorable conversion rates. Social enterprises that offered digital work to refugees and crisis-affected people in Lebanon were forced to circumvent the barriers to payment that refugees faced by channeling payments through local NGO partners. But individual refugees who worked online through larger digital labor platforms, without the support of enterprises and NGOs, did not have this possibility. The failures of the formal financial system and exclusion from major payment services fueled the rapid growth of the unregulated cryptocurrency market. Amid refugees' financial exclusion, stablecoins like USDT and other cryptocurrencies may offer an alternative way of storing value, making and receiving digital payments, or buying goods in informal peer-to-peer markets.[49]

"Barely making ends meet": The devaluation of digital work By March 2023, the Lebanese pound traded around 140,000 per US dollar, representing a loss of 98 percent of its value since 2019; official rates provided by the Central Bank's exchange platform have been adjusted continuously but have been lower than the informal market rate.[50] These gradual increases of the official rate, which dramatically devaluated the Lebanese pound in an effort to control the spiraling market rate, further drove up inflation of food items, utility bills, and other essential goods.[51] As the Lebanese currency lost its key function to store value reliably, the economy underwent gradual dollarization, a process that also requires a steady inflow of dollars to avoid collapse.[52] Earnings from remote work in foreign currency could therefore play an important part for the economy, but unfortunately, this was no longer feasible for most refugees at a time of deepening crisis. Where individuals did manage to maintain an income from digital work, it became worth less and less.

The average monthly income of around US$270 that Syrian and Lebanese workers at the social impact platforms and enterprises Taqadam and B.O.T. estimated for themselves was already low before the financial crisis started to bite. The Lebanese freelancer Nadine, who joined B.O.T. after finishing digital skills trainings, had worked on seven projects by July 2020, one of them commissioned by an insurance company that took between three and four months. "They gave us pictures of car accidents and a copy of the driving license of the person involved in the accident, and we would have to fill the required information by the insurance company using the driver's license," she explained. For between eight to nine hours of work a day on this project across four months, she made US$900, which she could only cash out in Lebanese pounds far below the market rate. Maya, another Lebanese freelancer at B.O.T., worked on projects checking Excel sheets for errors that took between two and three months, for which she was paid a total of US$550.

As these already low levels of pay were further devalued by the capital controls that enforced conversion rates below the market value, the workers struggled to make ends meet. For another project Maya did in summer 2020, spanning between forty and forty-five days of work, she got paid 1,800,000 LBP, which converted to around US$470 at the time. By March 2023, this would have been worth as little as US$13. Adding the rising costs of mobile broadband services and internet connectivity, all of this undermined the feasibility of using digital work as a lifeline in times of crisis.

The income these self-employed digital workers reported would have been low even compared to the old official monthly minimum wage of 675,000 LBP, which equaled around US$450 at the officially pegged currency conversion rate before the crisis. Currency devaluation turned Lebanon's real minimum wage into one of the lowest in the world, at one point worth a mere US$24.[53] A devalued local currency, soaring inflation, and barriers faced by refugees without USD accounts made online freelancing and remote work less and less feasible the more the crisis intensified. Ziad, a graduate of a programming school, said in April 2021, "I am barely making ends meet with these small freelance projects that I manage to get. I can barely cover my own expenses. If the LBP rate was still as before, at 1,500 LBP, I would be able to support my family. But at this rate, there's no way I can do that."

This downward spiral added to the economic vulnerability that spread in the population. As the Syrian digital skills training graduate Rashid said about the impact of the crisis on his livelihood, "My situation was bad even before the economic crisis and corona [pandemic]. With this situation . . . I have no words, to be honest. If we had a bit of a chance to get by before, now we have nothing. I need to work anything . . . just to be able to make ends meet. Now, if I even hear about a new training opportunity, I might not even have the chance to go because I cannot afford not to work anymore." Raed, a twenty-nine-year-old Syrian graduate of a digital skills training program, further underlined the severity of the situation for Syrian households, saying, "*Alhamdullilah* we are living each day on its own. Trying to survive."

Findings from surveys illustrated the increasing levels of economic vulnerability. In the survey of freelancers working with the language service provider NaTakallam, a third of the fifteen Lebanon-based workers, who were asked about the impact of the economic crisis on their livelihood, stated they had to borrow money from family members or friends. The survey of graduates of the DST program conducted in 2021, with thirteen Syrian and sixteen Lebanese respondents, found that 32 percent accumulated debts at a grocery store, while 42 percent had to borrow money from friends or family, and 45 percent had to sell personal items for money to survive economically. Four respondents said they were struggling to pay for internet connection. Overall, these economic vulnerabilities were higher among Syrian than Lebanese graduates: 62 percent of Syrians had to borrow money from friends or family compared to 31 percent of Lebanese; 54 percent of Syrians accumulated debt at a grocery compared with 19 percent of Lebanese; and all four respondents who struggled to pay for internet connection were Syrian.

Against this backdrop, the crisis further worsened the precarity of insecure digital work with the added risk of accumulating debt. This was particularly worrying, as already vulnerable refugees took financial risks and invested into training courses that ultimately did not lead to the expected job outcomes. Bilal, a graduate of the DST program, said in March 2021, "After I lost my job and joined the trainings, I started selling my furniture to make ends meet. I was okay making this sacrifice because I thought that by the end of the trainings, I will be able to start working and make up all what I had lost." These experiences raise concern about the promotion of precarious self-employed work that lacks any social protections and often demands unpaid labor time and investments without secure returns.

Benefits against all odds Despite challenges and precarious conditions, Syrian and Lebanese workers also underlined the importance of digital livelihoods for their economic survival. A survey of thirty freelancers working with the social impact platforms and enterprises Taqadam and B.O.T. showed that digital work was the only source of income for 80 percent of respondents, which underlines its economic significance. More than two-thirds considered their digital work as "extremely important" for their economic survival, with the rest seeing it at least as "very important." At NaTakallam, 60 percent of the fifteen surveyed workers who were based in Lebanon noted that without their income from selling remote language services, they would not be able to pay for food, rent, or basic services. For the mostly well-educated Lebanese workers who still managed to cash out freshly earned dollars during the financial crisis, this became an important contribution to their household's economic survival. Online freelance work could thereby provide some "stability in the presence of market collapse and the tools required to withstand periods of domestic economic turmoil."[54]

Tamer, a Lebanese graduate of a coding school, talked about the significance of online income opportunities and payments in USD for his family at a time of crisis:

> My dad and my brother lost their jobs. So, I was super lucky that I got to start my job just in time to help my family. It really affected us financially because my dad was the main provider for the family and then he was no longer able to provide. My brother also, he was able to cover his own expenses but not anymore. The fact that I was getting paid in fresh dollars really helped especially with the devaluation of the Lebanese lira. It compensated a bit.

In addition to this financial contribution, digital livelihood programs offered wider social and personal benefits to participants. The team that led the DST program at AUB emphasized the benefits of bringing young Syrian and Lebanese youth together on a regular basis to learn digital skills. DST participants surveyed after training completion consistently expressed increased self-confidence, such as one Syrian refugee who did not know how to operate a mouse on the first day of training and proudly presented a web development project six months later.[55] The trainings also inspired some to continue their education: A Syrian woman stated that digital skills training inspired her to study office management and accounting after a long period of depression and social disconnection following a divorce. The DST program also aimed to increase "social cohesion" between Syrian and Lebanese participants, with more than 90 percent of surveyed participants stating they developed friendships with peers of diverse backgrounds.[56]

One of the DST managers, Sarah, emphasized the specific benefits the program brought to refugee women, who were often unable to find suitable work and develop their skills. "Many young women, initially, they just want to do something and get out of home and get the money. But some get so excited and motivated," said Sarah. However, that this excitement often had to give way to disappointment was especially disempowering for these young Syrian women, who often had very few alternatives. Although the many benefits of digital livelihood programs are important in their own right, they do not change the disastrous impact of refugees' multilayered exclusion from a digital economy, which—as we have seen earlier—left many of the motivated students unable to convert the skills they learned into actual employment outcomes.

Conclusion: The Digital Exile of Syrian Refugees in Crisis-Affected Lebanon

Lebanon was both a birthplace and a deathbed for digital livelihood initiatives supporting refugees. It was here that leading humanitarian organizations such as the WFP and UNICEF partnered with social enterprises and educators to develop and test new experimental approaches to supporting refugees with digital skills and work. The founder of NaTakallam, Aline Sara, first developed the idea for a platform that connects refugees to paying language learners in response to the Syrian refugee crisis in Lebanon.[57] Some of the first digital refugee workers who classified images to train data for AI also emerged from pioneering initiatives here. Although always highly challenging, the early journeys of these programs and enterprises were hopeful and promising: Digital platforms and remote work seemed to offer a new solution for refugees who arrived in the country, and especially for those who were young, motivated, and already relatively well educated but locally excluded from employment.

A more sobering reality soon replaced this early hype, as the liberatory potential of digital skills training and online work crumbled away in the face of refugees' systematic marginalization and a spiralling financial crisis. This underlines how the application of digital tools in humanitarian aid often replicates or amplifies complex layers of exclusion that restrict target populations on the ground.[58] While the digital livelihoods approach theoretically offers economic opportunities for refugees that lie outside of a restrictive local context, it cannot transcend the multiple sources of economic, financial, political, and digital exclusion that affect refugees in Lebanon. Viewed from their perspective, the digital economy was unable to bridge the very "ruptures" that define a state of *crisis*—the "critical condition or conjuncture"[59] of displacement and economic collapse that created a need for the intervention in the first place. Lebanon's multiple crises further undermined the already limited digital economic opportunities at the time when people needed them most. All of this unmasks an ostensibly inclusive digital economy as a failed experiment of humanitarian innovation, one that is ultimately unfit to offer refugees accessible and secure employment opportunities in this particularly challenging context.

The causes behind this failure are manifold. National policies excluded Syrian refugees from employment and from digital work opportunities, while regulations and policies limited their access to digital platforms and financial services. The economic crisis led to further financial restrictions and to the devaluation of the money earned through work. Unlike the universal impact of the financial and economic crisis, Syrian refugees' exclusion from digital training and work opportunities was highly discriminatory and targeted. Their experience exemplifies how a digital economy can become yet another site in which forcibly displaced people are turned into outcasts: as exiles who are relegated to the margins of the digital economy at the national and the transnational level. As they are either excluded from a digital economy or precariously included in it, the digital exile they experience involves ongoing forms of confinement and restriction that are based on their status as forcibly displaced people.[60] Their economic exclusion and rightlessness at the national level is mirrored by the regulatory exclusion and marginalization in a global digital marketplace.

The regional conflict and volatile political environment that followed the economic crisis in Lebanon further undermined the capacity of a digital economy to support refugees and host community members during times of crisis. As the escalating Gaza War in 2023 spilled over into a conflict between Hezbollah and Israel, Israel also employed tactics of "digital warfare": alongside digital surveillance and GPS spoofing, its military attacks disrupted connectivity and damaged telecommunications infrastructures, which have already been weakened by the country's economic and financial collapse. Connectivity not only became disrupted but also more expensive, as people relied on mobile data in the face of digital infrastructure failure.[61] The impact of violent conflict, political instability, and digital warfare only added major challenges to the already difficult lives of those who aspired to benefit from a digital economy in Lebanon.

The other major event that raised new questions about the future role of digital economies for Syrian refugees in Lebanon was the fall of the Assad regime in December 2024. The unexpectedly rapid downfall followed a sustained military campaign by opposition forces and prompted many European governments to halt Syrian asylum applications and start thinking about voluntary and forced returns. The Lebanese Prime Minister Najib Mikati was equally quick in calling on Syrians to return home, stating that "the strain on our resources has been substantial, worsening existing economic trouble and creating fierce competition for jobs and services."[62] Once and if the Syrian economy stabilizes and international sanctions are lifted, returnees from Lebanon and elsewhere in the world, who were trained in digital skills and gained digital work experience, may play a crucial role in such economic recovery. However, the massive infrastructure damage inflicted by more than a decade of conflict, as well as underdeveloped and fragmented digital systems, combined with sanctions to lock Syrians out of digital opportunities and services, continuing to prevent its "digital recovery."[63]

2
Online Freelancing Among Refugees in Kenya

Bounded Liberation and Digital Risks in the Gig Economy

I met the twenty-nine-year-old Somali Abdi in Nairobi's Westlands area, an affluent residential neighborhood that is home to major hotels and office buildings. Although living in the Eastleigh neighborhood on the other side of the highway, he suggested we meet in a café of the spacious Westlands shopping mall.

"My life was that of a refugee," he said when I asked him about his past. He was born "on the way" in a temporary refugee settlement at the border and spent the rest of his youth in the Dadaab camp, where his family still lived. Now he was a successful interpreter and translator who built a good reputation on freelancing platforms and worked with humanitarian organizations. His exposure to digital technology started after high school, when he worked as a teacher with an organization that offered training in digital skills. "That's when I got interested in freelancing," he said. In 2014, friends showed him how he could make money remotely with Somali-English transcription work and helped him set up his own account with the platform Appen. It was the beginning of a journey that exemplifies how the digital economy can support forcibly displaced people to make an income from remote work, contributing to what Abdi saw as a shift from the life "of a refugee" to a life of economic independence and professional success.

Succeeding in making money online was not easy, however. As an independent contractor with Appen, he had to take frequent assessments, saying, "You read some manuals, do some tests, and when they see you follow instructions, they review it, give you feedback, and if you go above the required threshold for quality, then you are good to work. There is an assessment after every project you work." One job was doing audio transcriptions of phone calls, which were split into 30-to-60-second segments and then distributed to contractors like him, who got paid per segment. He never knew who contracted the work. "This was confidential," he said. "The job was just to sign in, click on those jobs, transcribe the audios—nothing else." The pay was not great, but for a newcomer, "that rate wasn't bad for us," he said. This was especially so from the perspective of a skilled refugee who lived in a camp without adequate employment opportunities.

After a few months of freelance transcription work, he was without work for three years. He said that Appen then offered new jobs in annotations to train AI models, and he managed to pass the screening and was onboarded once again. This time, his job was to collect the links for YouTube videos on different topics, "then we take the link and play the video in a system they created. Then you truncate the video: introduction, news break, you define the topic . . . truncate it, label it: politics, education, and so on." After a few months, the work dried up again. It was a highly insecure livelihoods resource. Asked about this insecurity, Abdi said, "That's the problem of that side of freelancing. You have a source of job for a moment, but you never know when this source will stop. Clients who give consistent projects for a time, they enjoy, and then they disappear." Eventually he got a scholarship to study at university and moved to Nairobi while continuing freelance translation work remotely.

Although insecurity remains one of its distinguishing features, the rapid spread of online freelance work in Kenya has offered growing numbers of workers an important source of income generation. As the story of Abdi shows, online freelancing has played a particularly important role for skilled refugees who live in refugee camps without sufficient job opportunities. Amid a digital economy that contributes around 10 percent of Kenya's GDP,[1] the number of online gig workers in the country may have reached more than a million.[2] The Ajira Digital Program, which wants to turn the country into a global digital freelancing hub, at one point even referred to "over 1.9 million Kenyans working online."[3] How reliable these numbers are is unclear. Capturing the exact number of online gig workers in Kenya is certainly difficult, as many accounts are held by individuals who outsource work to others, while some share accounts, hide their identities, or use fake ones. Even so, Kenya had the fourth-largest share of online freelance workers in the field of writing and translation globally between 2023 and 2024, supplying 7 percent of the total global workforce in this field on major online labor platforms.[4] Other prominent fields of online freelance work in Kenya are editing services, business services, IT and data analytics, and creative and professional services.[5]

This trend is further underpinned by the spread and growth of digital labor platforms: By 2024, there were some 88 online freelance platforms, 25 microtask platforms, and 29 remote tutoring platforms active in Kenya, as well as some 180 location-based platforms spanning a diversity of services such as taxi, delivery, domestic work, and health-care services.[6] Such growth has been supported by wider investments into connectivity, infrastructure, data centers, entrepreneurship and innovation, digital skills development and coding schools, and a digital financial ecosystem where mobile money and fintech platforms are integrated into digital labor platforms to allow "seamless" transfers.[7] However, this "seamlessness" of digital transactions rarely applies to refugees in Kenya, many of whom continue to face a myriad of barriers and challenges.

This chapter explores the precarious inclusion of refugees into a transnational digital economy against the backdrop of Kenya's wider digital transformation and its restrictive regulation of forced displacement. A particular focus lies on the role of the digital economy for refugees who live in the confinement of camps, questioning to what extent the boundary-transcending hypermobility of online work can liberate, or virtually mobilize, forcibly displaced people from the entrapment and limitations of their local condition. Their experiences with the digital economy involve a range of challenges and risks that highlight the disempowering effects of their digital economic inclusion, in addition to the effects of their exclusion by ways of policies, laws, and regulations. This perspective builds on the notion of "adverse digital incorporation" to explore "the inequalities that arise in the global South when less-advantaged individuals and groups are included in rather than simply excluded from digital systems."[8] From the perspective of refugees, such unequal effects of digital incorporation include a set of challenges and risks that show how the wider inequalities affecting refugees are deepened and reconfigured within the wider digital economy.

Refugees in Kenya: The Wider Context

Kenya hosted some 836,905 refugees and asylum seekers by 2025. More than half were from Somalia, and some 32 percent from South Sudan, alongside major refugee populations from DRC, Ethiopia, Burundi, and Sudan. Some 86 percent of refugees resided in the Garissa and Turkana regions that host the two major refugee camp complexes of Dadaab and Kakuma/Kalobeyei, and some 13 percent of registered refugees and asylum seekers were based in Nairobi.[9] The Employment Act 2019 provides all legal residents in Kenya with the right to work, and the Refugees Act of 2021 states specifically that refugees have the right to work.

However, access to this right is limited in practice, as refugees need permits to work legally. Applying for a so-called "Class M" permit is a difficult process with insecure outcomes that requires documents, such as an official refugee ID and tax registration, which can pose challenges for refugees. Additionally, employers are required to justify why they would hire a refugee over a Kenyan.[10] The Refugees Act also establishes the right for self-employment, and refugees who engage in self-employed work or business activities, including online freelance workers, need to register with the tax authorities. Applying for a business license comes with bureaucratic barriers too, although the application process is experienced as more effective, and the outcomes tend to be more positive, than with work permits.[11]

In addition to the challenges of obtaining permits, refugees' capacity to become economically active is limited by movement restrictions. Although the Kenyan constitution grants every person the right to freedom of movement, the Refugees Act and the government's policies restrict the freedom of movement for refugees who are confined to designated camps and must obtain a movement pass if they wish to travel outside these areas.[12] While movement passes for medical reasons and education are frequently provided, workers or business owners are often not allowed to move beyond the boundaries of a camp. This is one of the reasons why only around 7.5 percent of refugees in the Dadaab camp were economically active.[13]

Online freelance work theoretically offers unique opportunities to virtually transcend these mobility restrictions and bureaucratic obstacles. Unfortunately, difficulties in obtaining and renewing official refugee IDs, which are needed not only to obtain permits but also to register with platforms and financial services, have undermined the digital economy's potential as an inclusive livelihood resource.[14]

Another factor that influences the feasibility of making a digitally enabled livelihood is location. Refugees living in cities have access to faster and more reliable internet connectivity and may benefit from other infrastructures, such as co-working spaces. Refugee households' average income per capita is also significantly higher in cities than in camps,[15] making it more likely they can afford smartphones, internet connectivity, and computers. Some computer-equipped centers from which refugees can go online and develop their skills, or even work remotely, do exist in camps. However, electricity and internet connectivity remain restricted and not available at all times. At the same time, refugees living outside of camps in Nairobi often do so unofficially and therefore lack access to the recognized IDs they would need to work online.

The inequalities between national refugee groups are another factor that influences individual capacities to benefit from a digital economy. In Kakuma, the more recently arrived South Sudanese have close to nothing and are substantially worse off than other nationalities, often relying on food aid, and in Nairobi, Somali refugees are significantly better off and have higher incomes than the Congolese.[16] Different refugee nationalities can also develop their own specializations in the digital economy, such as Somali refugees working as freelance translators and interpreters. Despite a myriad of challenges, online freelance work has emerged as a powerful aspiration especially among those refugees in Kenya who live in camps and are relatively well educated and lack adequate local employment opportunities. Yet, their voices are absent from the wider digital transformation policies and processes that have reshaped the country's economy.

Refugees at the Margins of Digital Transformation

Refugees' incorporation into a digital economy needs to be understood in the wider context of digital transformation in Kenya, which prioritizes citizens and defines economic development in national terms. Kenya and other African countries have framed digital technology as a pathway to overcome their peripheral economic position and leapfrog across developmental stages.[17] The stated mission of Kenya's Digital Economy Blueprint, for example, is to become "a nation where every citizen, enterprise and organization has digital access and the capability to participate and thrive in the digital economy," while acknowledging that the "digital economy offers Kenya a leapfrogging opportunity on economic development."[18] Kenya is recognized as a digital pioneer and role model for other African states that envision a similar transformation, even if they still have a long way to go. Take, for example, Kenya's poorer neighbors Uganda and Ethiopia, which are among the world's Least Developed Countries (LDCs). Although both countries invest high hopes into the benefits of digital transformation in their respective national strategies and visions, only 10.3 percent of the population in Uganda and 16.7 percent in Ethiopia used the internet (compared with 41 percent in Kenya).[19] Yet, as this chapter will show from the viewpoint of refugees, Kenya's wider success in promoting digital inclusion and connectivity hides the many barriers to *meaningful* connectivity, which would provide everyone with a safe, satisfying, enriching, productive, and affordable online experience.[20]

In line with refugees' exclusion from the nation's identity and their confinement to designated camps, they are equally marginalized in the government's wider digital transformation policies and strategies, despite important local initiatives that support them in developing digital skills and finding work. These initiatives are often funded by aid agencies and collaborate with enterprises and digital platforms while promoting the idea that digital technology is key to addressing the developmental and humanitarian problems that affect forcibly displaced people. However, participants of these programs often struggle to convert learning into earning, as they frequently lack access to computers and receive insufficient ongoing support to become successful independently and build a track record on platforms.[21]

A lack of such support is at least partly because refugees' needs are widely overlooked by Kenya's digital transformation policies and initiatives, which include a Kenya National ICT Masterplan, a National Broadband Strategy, the National Digital Masterplan 2022–2032, and a national Digital Literacy Programme, among others. The Digital Economy Blueprint, which seeks to promote an "inclusive" digital economy, explicitly focuses on *citizens* and only mentions the term "refugees" once. Although the government has emphasized the need for digital transformation of a wide demography across the country, refugees are invisible in these official policies and considerations.[22] Indirectly, some of the challenges they face may be reflected in general statements toward equality and inclusion. For example, the Digital Masterplan advocates for digital inclusion across demographic divides, acknowledging the specific needs of youth, women, minorities, the elderly, rural communities, and persons with disability. Some of the stated challenges that perpetuate digital exclusion among these marginalized groups equally apply to refugees. They include cost of access, skills, lack of content, poor connectivity, information gaps and limited mobility, and limited ownership and control of digital devices, as well as safety and security concerns.[23]

Rather than supporting the digital inclusion of minorities, many of the Kenyan government's regulations of the sector have focused on extracting revenues from platforms and workers. The government introduced a 16 percent value-added tax (VAT) on mobile phones and SIM cards, in addition to a 12 percent transaction fee for mobile money, which added to the lack of affordability of mobile phones and services, a main barrier to digital inclusion.[24] A Finance Act passed in 2022 applied a 1.5 percent tax on digital services such as online advertising, digital audio/video content, and services provided by platform workers in the online gig economy, and in 2023, Kenya imposed a 16 percent VAT on all payments of the global freelance giant Upwork, which ended up being deducted from workers' earnings.

The regulations and taxation imposed on both platforms and workers have created new barriers for refugees in Kenya, many of whom have long been active on Upwork and a range of other platforms. The difficulties refugees face in obtaining the necessary tax registrations are well illustrated in an Upwork community forum post titled "Inability to Provide Tax Information on Upwork Due to Lack of KRA Pin for Refugees." The user writes that they are currently residing in Kakuma Refugee Camp and hold a refugee ID, being "a registered refugee in Kenya": "I am having difficulty accessing tax policy in Kenya, specifically the Kenya Revenue Authority Pin (KRA Pin). . . . Unfortunately, this constraint is preventing me from withdrawing my earnings from Upwork. . . . I appreciate your prompt attention to this issue and look forward to your guidance on how to proceed."[25]

This example of regulations' tangible impact on refugees who seek to work on digital labor platforms shows that they must shoulder the worst aspects of both informality and formalization: The few formal rules that govern the sector only seem to make it harder for them to take part in a digital economy, rather than supporting and protecting them; and the precarity of online gig work, as an insecure form of self-employment, only continues the already prevalent trend of informal and unprotected labor.

Gig Work Nation

Not only refugees but also Kenyan digital workers have been literally left to their own devices. The rapid emergence of an online gig economy has outpaced efforts to protect citizens and workers through appropriate policies, laws, and regulations. As the digital platform economy in Kenya continues to grow, it will be crucial that workers—including refugees—are better protected and that exploitative labor practices are exposed and addressed. Owing in part to a lack of regulations and worker protections, most digital labor platforms in Kenya score poorly in the ratings by the Fairwork Foundation, which creates scores for platforms based on pay, conditions, contracts, management, and representation.[26] The harmful conditions of online freelance work in Kenya were also brought into international spotlight by a range of lawsuits against Meta.

One of these lawsuits, which also targeted Meta's subcontractor for content moderation, Sama, highlighted the problematic treatment of workers, as well as violations of their rights and rock-bottom wages.[27] The case was brought to the courts by a former worker, who was hired as a Facebook content moderator through Sama and was allegedly "exposed to graphic and traumatic content at work, without adequate prior knowledge or proper psychosocial support—which he says left him with post-traumatic stress disorder."[28] *The Economist* magazine reported on the lawsuits, stating, "They all concern the invisible army of moderators used by tech firms to cleanse their platforms of violent or illegal content. Together the cases illuminate the grim reality for low-paid African workers of the global tech boom."[29] The death of a Nigerian content moderator in March 2025 who worked for a subcontractor of TikTok fueled further outrage over precarious working conditions.[30] She was reportedly desperate to return home but unable to do so, while being locked into exploitative and unsupported working conditions without a permit. These developments raise concern about the suitability of digital jobs and gig work for forcibly displaced people, who are more likely to remain invisible, are therefore easily exploitable, and enter the digital economy with a range of preexisting vulnerabilities and risks.

Although the digital dimension of a gig economy is relatively new, the notion of "gig work" is far from alien in a country where the vast majority of workers are employed in the informal sector. The platform economy has therefore become the digital extension of an already prevalent informal labor market: Informal employment as a proportion of total employment in Kenya rose from 10 percent in 1974 to 83 percent in 2019, and by 2021, nine in ten workers in the informal economy were in informal microenterprises, largely without access to national security and unionization, with estimated average wages below the minimum wage.[31] The high proportion of young people who are looking for work has contributed to the rapid growth of the online gig economy, which is often seen as an innovative alternative to the lack of decent employment opportunities.[32] For many, it has also become a crucial lifeline for familial and communal financial support, as more than 70 percent of platform workers in Kenya surveyed in a study said they were providing financial support to individuals outside of their immediate households.[33]

The concept of "hustling" is often used to describe the prevalence of working across several jobs and gigs, as a defining survival strategy of marginalized urban workers that has come to define senses of national identity and solidarity.[34] While the more idealized notion of "the hustle" emphasizes hard work and creative innovation, it equally expresses the injustice of "economic systems that offload risk onto individual workers, particularly workers already marginalized within the dominant society."[35] Refugees' experience with self-employed platform work offers a particular variety of this combination of hard work, innovation, and marginalization, one that remains outside of dominant discourses about hustling as a marker of Kenyan national identity. We will see that the digital economy has liberatory potential by providing remote work for refugees who are entrapped in camps and restricted by regulations. At the same time, the potential for such work to provide a reliable, safe, and sustainable source of employment that would contribute to self-reliance is held at bay by additional layers of restriction, entrapment, and insecurity that define their experience in this digital refugee economy.

Bounded Liberation: Online Freelancing from a Refugee Camp

The twenty-three-year-old Somali refugee Abshir went to primary and secondary school in the Dadaab camp before joining a training course in digital skills aimed at empowering refugees to make money in online freelance work. Such online freelancing was "the only way to earn an income" in Dadaab, said Abshir, adding that "in online work, you have to be responsible on your own and provide everything you can to be successful. You have to be very mature and very attentive." He contrasted the benefits of this demanding remote work with the lack of suitable local jobs, saying that in the camp, one may not find a suitable job opportunity for months. "Online, you see opportunities all the time," he added.

Viewed from the restricted space of a refugee camp, the abundance of jobs posted on online freelancing platforms comes to represent a seemingly infinite world of opportunities. Underpinned by a range of initiatives that promote online freelance work as a way out of local restrictions and spatial limitations, the digital economy gains a powerful liberatory potential that resonates strongly among refugees. As they struggle to overcome a myriad of barriers, they come to symbolize what Andrew Leon Hanna calls "the most extreme entrepreneurs on the planet," who "face greater obstacles than perhaps any other class of entrepreneurs."[36] Succeeding in establishing oneself as a successful entrepreneur, or a freelance worker, from one of the world's largest refugee camps is indeed a tremendous achievement. Their susceptibility to the dreams and hopes that a digital economy instills in them can only be understood in relation to the restrictions they face as refugees living in camps.

Meeting the Demand for Highly Skilled Workers

The many barriers that stand between the abundance of opportunities in a digital economy and aspiring refugee workers' ambitions include a wide gap in digital skills and education. The level of education among online freelancers can seem intimidatingly high: Some 61 percent of men and 56 percent of women reported having a university degree in a survey of 284 online freelance workers in Kenya.[37] On web-based digital labor platforms in Kenya, which include online freelance, microtask, and tutoring platforms, as well as remote outsourcing work, most workers either have a university degree (between 41 percent and 58 percent, depending on the type of platform) or were pursuing a degree (between 30 percent and 40 percent).[38] This can be contrasted with 84 percent of refugees between the age of twenty-five and sixty-four in Garissa County, which hosts the Dadaab refugee complex, never having attended school, according to a UN survey.[39] Refugees living in cities tend to have much higher educational levels than those who remain in camps.[40] This wide gap between individual capabilities and demand illustrates the crucial importance of skills development as a key enabler of refugees' inclusion in a digital economy. A range of initiatives and programs led by aid organizations and the private sector strived to fill this gap.

One of them was a program led by the Kenya Private Sector Alliance (KEPSA) and Amahoro Coalition in Dadaab and Kakuma, which offered free digital skill training and mentorship opportunities to connect refugees to income opportunities in the digital economy.[41] Perhaps the most well-known initiative that brought digital skills and online freelancing to refugees in Kenya's camps has been run by the Norwegian Refugee Council (NRC) and the International Trade Centre (ITC) under the name Refugee Employment and Skills

Initiative (RESI), a program that later morphed into a new consortium under the name of Area-Based Livelihood Initiative in Garissa. By 2021, RESI had trained some 450 refugee youths and helped connect them to work and entrepreneurship opportunities. Its main avenue for job placement was the Dadaab Collective Freelancing Agency. As an agency registered with the platform Upwork, it mediated between refugees and clients as an umbrella organization, having sourced work from many international clients, including tech giants such as Amazon.[42]

Abshir was one of the program's beneficiaries, having managed to build on training courses and other support to become a successful online freelancer selling language services through digital platforms. As someone who completed secondary school and prepared to study information technology at university, his story indicates that digital livelihoods initiatives often benefit the highly motivated and most well educated. As Mercy, a project assistant working for the Norwegian Refugee Council in Dadaab, explained, "We need youths who can communicate freely because they deal with clients outside Kenya. They need good communication skills. It restricts us to select only youths who finished high school and can communicate easily and freely. Not many of the youths have been to high school, there are many dropouts. So, the challenge is to get these youths into the program."

Navigating Connectivity Restrictions

Getting access to digital skills courses is only the first step in a series of challenges, many of which surface as part of the work experience the programs enable. Asked about his usual work experience, Abshir highlighted some of the challenges this work involved: "Normally, I go online for most of my time, although there is a limit to the internet here. I go to a local center for internet and power, which is also limited. It's quite challenging. At least I can manage to go online for most of the day to look for jobs and apply. If I get an interview, then I do the job and complete it. Deadlines can be tight."

The problem of unreliable internet connectivity makes clear how the liberatory potential of a transnational digital economy remains bounded by the local inequalities and restrictions that forcibly displaced people face in camps. "The internet situation is difficult here. Not everyone can afford the [data] bundles to access the internet. Without internet, you cannot be an online freelancer. You miss all the jobs you could have applied for," said Abshir. Even for those who managed to pay for mobile data or used the computer-equipped centers in the camp, time-restricted internet and electricity provision contributed to a highly disruptive and insecure work experience. Abdullahi, another experienced online freelancer and mentor in the Dadaab freelancing agency, explained the problem in the following way:

> They created centers where, in daytime, freelancers can come together to do the work. There were accessibility problems because maybe the watchman is never there, or doesn't allow everyone in, or there is no internet, no power. And at night, which is when we freelancers normally apply for jobs, because it's when they post the jobs in the US, in the West, so, if you don't have a laptop and data bundles and internet, you have all these kinds of problems. And the power issues: In Dadaab, we have generators run by refugee camp members, at 9 a.m. the power comes, and at 12 it goes off. At 3 or 4, it comes back on and then it goes off at 6, comes back at 7, goes off again at 10. They are operating it to preserve the engine while providing electricity. But if you need it at night, there is nothing you can do.

This complicated experience in navigating the limitations of internet connectivity in the camp underlines how refugees' marginalization at the local level is reinforced by a digital economy at the transnational level. Sporadic and unreliable internet connectivity severely affects refugees' capacity to access digital income opportunities despite the existence of training centers and internet cafes.[43] This presents "a staggering barrier to accessing digital work opportunities" in Kenya's refugee camps.[44] Other widespread barriers to connectivity include the cost of data, poor network signal strength, the high cost of phones, and the difficulty in charging them, as well as poor digital literacy.[45] These combined challenges express a tension at the heart of the digital refugee economy in Kenya: that online and remote work are only liberatory insofar as they offer access to money and web-based markets while failing to address the underlying inequalities and systematic layers of marginalization and spatial confinement. In many ways, the digital economy mirrors their marginalization at the local and national level. Emblematic of this was how refugee online freelancers felt compelled to hide their location, their refugee status, and their origin from their online presence. "My profile is still set to Nairobi," said Abdullahi, adding, "That's where I created it from. Even when I was in Somalia, I landed some jobs. These jobs, I never told the client I am in Somalia. I never changed my profile location."

Navigating the Challenges of Online Gig Work

Those who aspired to make a livelihood through online freelance work faced the double burden of having to navigate the restrictions they faced as refugees alongside the challenges of insecure and precarious gig work. When Abshir did not actively work on a project, he would often spend up to ten hours a day searching and applying for jobs—all unpaid labor time. Alongside his regular translation work, Abshir sometimes did basic data entry jobs to get by, which were usually badly paid. "You cannot get a job daily. Once in a week, you maybe get a job, or three to four times a month. But in the end, the earnings support you. Sometimes I don't even get a job every week," he said. However insecure these income streams from gig work may be, online freelancing comes to represent a new imaginary of success and liberation for forcibly displaced people who have long been relegated to informal and insecure jobs at the margins of national economies.

Abdullahi from Somalia was a highly successful role model for aspiring refugee freelancers, a living emblem for the possibilities of "extreme entrepreneurship." After finishing school in Dadaab, he worked as a primary school teacher with an aid organization for $70 a month. He started to consider online freelance work with the platform Appen in 2014, when "people talked a lot about it." His eventual success was partly due to his strong determination. When Abdullahi first heard about a training course for online freelancers in Nairobi by the Danish Refugee Council, he called them up straightaway and asked if he could join. Although he was initially rejected because he lived in Dadaab, outside of the course's catchment area, he convinced them to let him join "off the record," as he put it. "I used the money I had in my pocket and went there," he said. The five-day training was held in a hotel in Nairobi and involved hands-on work experience with the impact sourcing enterprise Sama Source (now Sama).

He then had to invest resources and time into growing his reputation as a translator on freelancing platforms. "The first time I started to create my account on Upwork . . . I said, let me try if languages actually work. I didn't land a job for the first few months, but one came in after that for five dollars. What I wanted was a reputation, the feedback," he explained. Weeks or months of bidding for the first few jobs was not unusual, and this system heavily prioritized either those who already had positive profile reviews and a track record of job completion, or those who offered their services at lower rates than others. Those who had a track record of positive reviews and low rates gained a competitive advantage. The need to get some positive reviews incentivizes newcomers to do jobs for very little money, or even for no pay at all. This can be a real problem for refugees who already lived in highly precarious financial situations and invest their time and resources into gig work that offers no guarantee of financial returns.

Adding to this insecurity and the financial burden was the cost of high-end computers and software that translators like Abdullahi needed. A program he used for translation cost US$2,600, or at least hundreds of dollars per year on a subscription basis, he said. The high-speed laptop he needed cost him $1,600. While early phases of the digital livelihood programs in Dadaab offered laptops for participants, this was later restricted to those who already demonstrated success in getting paid online work. "But for you to show that success, you have to have a laptop in the first place. That was a gap," said Abdullahi. Additional costs involved in online freelancing are the subscription fees of platforms, and in the case of Upwork, the costs of so-called "Connects" that are required by workers to submit and "boost" their proposal for job postings. This business model increasingly excludes or threatens potential online workers from economically marginalized backgrounds, such as refugees, who are in no position to take financial risks.

The challenges and costs associated with gig work on major freelancing platforms are one reason why translators like Abshir, Abdi, and Abdullahi gradually shifted to alternative platforms such as ProZ, which is a different kind of membership-based platform for freelance translators. The founder of ProZ, Henry Dotterer, emphasized in a remote interview that their approach was different from other major freelancing platforms: "We don't take a commission. . . . Our model is to work for the translator, not the client. Our customer is the service provider, not the customer paying. We work for the Uber drivers. It's an inverted model." There was no "auction style" bidding process and no hidden cost outside of the yearly membership plan. They were committed to supporting refugees and allocated a special department that tried to work out feasible payment solutions with workers in challenging local settings. A collaboration with another platform also provided job opportunities in live remote translation services to various clients, including hospitals. By 2021, they had more than one hundred refugees working as remote interpreters from Kenya, according to their estimate.

Another strategy for refugees to mitigate the challenges of exploitative digital labor platforms was the creation of the Dadaab Collective Freelancing Agency, which supported workers in acquiring projects and offered some cushioning between them and the highly competitive digital labor market. When the agency sourced projects from clients, it distributed them to refugee workers, who then delivered the work, while the agency took a commission of 10 percent from their earnings to enable its continuing support. Aided by skills development and mentorship arrangements, such an agency can be successful in creating independent income streams for individual refugees while allowing greater coordination and representation on a collective level. As such, the agency and its associated training program supported refugees in navigating the challenges and insecurities of online freelance work.

Several other refugee-serving initiatives set up agencies on digital platforms in this way. The Somali refugee Mohammed, who started out freelancing through the Dadaab collective, later launched his own agency called Desert Freelancing Agency. It functioned as a "collective online work account" that allowed him and his peers to bid for work as a company through Upwork and redistribute these jobs to some fifty workers in the camp.[46] The agency was not only a way to avoid restrictions on registering a business locally, but it also allowed successful pioneers like Mohammed to leverage good reviews and reputation for the benefit of others, who would otherwise struggle to succeed while starting from scratch. This indicates that online freelance work, which is commonly described as highly individualized and isolating, can develop its own redistributive dynamic through innovative ways of organizing refugee workers from below.

While unable to change the insecure character of platform work, the development of alternative models of organizing and support in camps became both a necessity and an opportunity. It was needed to overcome barriers and mitigate the disempowering effects of the online gig economy, and it presented an opportunity to redistribute the benefits from individual success among larger cohorts of less advanced beneficiaries who may otherwise remain excluded. However, these forms of intermediation between refugees and a digital economy primarily worked around and through challenges and barriers, without transforming the underlying inequalities that made them necessary in the first place.

Refugee Women at the Margins of a Digital Economy

Women are often disadvantaged compared to men at different stages of their journeys into a digital economy. This begins at the foundational level of mobile and internet connectivity, as men tend to have higher rates of internet access compared to women.[47] This gender gap is higher in mobile broadband usage than it is for mobile phone usage more generally.[48] On average, the gender gap is around 19 percent for mobile internet use and 17 percent for smartphone ownership in low- and middle-income countries. In Kenya, only 39 percent of women compared to 59 percent of men use mobile internet.[49] Women in Kenya are also less likely to own computers than men. These factors not only limit refugee women's ability to access and benefit from remote work but often also discourage them from considering it as an option in the first place.[50] Refugee women in Kenya who want to access digital work opportunities also face "cultural resistance" to their work as well as physical dangers when accessing computers and connectivity at night when most overseas jobs are posted on major freelancing platforms.[51]

As the experiences of Somali refugee women in Dadaab exemplify, a lack of affordable internet connectivity and computers often undermines the benefits that digital skills trainings could bring them. Halima, a twenty-five-year-old refugee in Dadaab, obtained an ICT Diploma and hoped to support her two children through remote freelance work. As a widow, she was in desperate need of an income. Working remotely only became a possibility when she received a start-up kit from the aid agency that delivered the training, which included a laptop, a mouse, and a headset. Now she was doing translation and interpretation work through the platform ProZ, mostly working "online at night," as she told me in a remote interview. She also tried to find jobs through Upwork, saying, "I do some work at Upwork. I did web research, data entry, voice over, and translation. I like Upwork, but the problem is when I apply for a job, they don't give me a chance to do the work." Out of fifteen jobs she applied for, she only got one.

Her work also suffered from a range of "technical network problems." Because of unreliable internet connectivity, she lost money and sometimes failed to complete jobs on time. She added, "The computer I am using now may get broken or something happens. I cannot afford to buy another laptop. They are very expensive in our area. I fear that if my laptop breaks, no one can help me and I will drop out of all the work I am doing now." She tried to make her work fit into the limited periods when internet was available in the camp, but she struggled to do so next to her familial obligations. She wanted to buy a solar panel for private electricity but could not afford it. Another problem she faced was the cost of data, which was especially high in the data-intensive translation and interpretation work she did. Out of the US$150–$200 of earnings per month that she estimated for herself, around $40 was spent on data, further decimating an already low income. "My main difficulty in terms of online freelancing is the data . . . so I struggle to earn more," she said. The need to charge devices posed another challenge even for those who owned smartphones or computers, as the majority of residents in Dadaab must charge their phones in kiosks for a fee or at their neighbor's home.[52]

With the little income she made, Halima supported her elder mother while "also helping my children and their education, clothes, food, health material, everything." Her story exemplifies how gender-related familial responsibilities combine with the wider precarity of gig work and connectivity barriers to undermine refugee women's capacity to benefit from the digital economy. With her family's entire livelihood hanging on a fine string, the laptop she received from an aid agency becomes the unstable foundation of a precarious economic lifeline.

Most refugees in Dadaab do not have a computer, and many were left without their own device after training completion. When I asked Fatima, another beneficiary of a digital livelihoods program in Kenya, about the main barriers she faced in accessing digital work, she said, "Most difficult is when you don't have a laptop like me. The job I would do, you must have a laptop. So, you need to find a neighbor who has a laptop if you don't have one. But those people who post the jobs, the clients, in foreign countries like America, they post them at a time that is midnight for us. This is the time during the day there. So, when you don't have a laptop, it's difficult."

Shouldering a Double Burden

The challenges Fatima faced in accessing online work opportunities did not dampen her hopes about the future. She said she would like to become an "expert online freelancer" who also serves her community; she wants to join university and study computer science. Speaking on a call after her return to Somalia, she said, "Now I am in Somalia, so I want to join university here when I get a good job." She perceived online freelancing to be perfectly suitable for women, as she explained, "Online work is the best because you can do your own dream online. You can build more knowledge, and you meet the whole world; you can work wherever you want, even when you become a mother and you can work from home next to your children and family." This exemplifies the powerful aspirations that remote freelance work engenders among refugees, suggesting a sense of freedom and flexibility that seems to be particularly suitable for mothers with home-based caring responsibilities.

At the same time, it is tremendously difficult to take care of a family and work online at the same time, resulting in a heavy double burden on aspiring female online freelancers who must balance multiple responsibilities. This becomes evident from an ILO survey of platform workers in Kenya, which showed that women experience unique challenges in balancing their work life and domestic responsibilities, which affects the number of hours they can do paid work: Women reported spending an average of six to eight hours in a typical day on domestic responsibilities, compared to four hours for men. Women platform workers often do not have anyone to help them with these additional responsibilities and therefore lack the flexibility to choose their working hours freely.[53] Women also generally earned less than men across most categories of online freelance work.[54]

This double burden can affect refugee women even more severely, despite many of them citing the ability to work from home as an important benefit. Yet even if refugee women made money online despite all these challenges, the digital economy exposed them to risks and harm: Refugee women in Kenya are "more likely to be subjected to harassment, increasing the stigma surrounding women building careers online."[55] However, as one study found, refugee women in Kenya can also perceive online work to be less risky than offline work, which made them feel more exposed to risks such as sexual exploitation.[56]

It did not help the hopeful journeys of aspiring refugee freelancers that the very digital incorporation of refugees that was enabled by supportive initiatives led to the emergence of a wide range of additional risks and challenges. These risks exemplify how the adverse digital incorporation of specific marginalized populations can deepen the inequalities and vulnerabilities they face.[57] As the restrictions imposed on refugees intersect with the precarity and insecurity of online freelance work, their participation in a digital economy becomes at once a source of economic benefit and of deepening precarity and risk.

The Risks of Refugee Online Work

On a September morning in 2022, a conference room in a Nairobi hotel slowly filled up with young men and women who had come to join a workshop about "staying safe while working online," which I organized with my colleague Margie Cheesman and UNHCR. Many of the young men and women who attended had completed digital skills training programs with organizations such as WUSC, RefuSHE, and Konexio, members of which took part in the workshop. Most of the participating refugees also had experience in doing online and remote work. Unfortunately, this also included their experience of the digital economy's dark side: a range of new risks and vulnerabilities that result from connectivity and digital inclusion, such as cybercrime and scams.[58] This included the risks that resulted from their attempts to circumvent barriers and exclusion with the help of precarious and informal workarounds.

Refugees are particularly vulnerable to digital risks: They must often use low-quality devices, may share mobile phones and computers with others, or access computers and go online in public community centers. Many refugee-hosting countries in the Global South also lack strong data protection and cybersecurity standards. Moreover, some refugee communities may lack the digital skills needed to identify and mitigate cybercrime. Many of the digital risks refugees in Kenya faced resulted from their exclusion from digital and financial services, due to challenges in obtaining recognized identification documents and because of laws and regulations. The prevalence of risk among beneficiaries of aid sector initiatives reveals how their incorporation into a digital economy can contradict the humanitarian sector's commitment to "doing no harm," with emerging digital approaches challenging guiding sets of principles and actions.[59] Digital livelihood programs and initiatives that are designed to support refugees often successfully connect them to a digital economy as intermediaries but subsequently fail to protect them from the resulting harm.[60]

Identification-Related Barriers and Emerging Risks

One key driver of risk among refugees who participate in a digital economy are the challenges of obtaining, maintaining, and recognizing their identity documents. In Kenya, these ID-related challenges exist for reasons such as a backlog in Refugee Status Determination and the resulting delays in IDs being issued, the exclusion of refugees in Nairobi from access to official registration and IDs, and backlogs during the renewal of IDs that is required every five years.[61] The lack of recognized identification can prevent refugees from accessing vital digital and financial services. As any customer of financial institutions and many other businesses, refugees in Kenya must satisfy KYC/Customer Due Diligence requirements, for which documents such as a birth certificate, a national ID card, and a driver's license or a passport is needed. Using a refugee ID for banking is not forbidden under Kenyan law, and advocacy has resulted in designated areas such as Kakuma and Dadaab being allowed to access banking with some institutions like Equity Bank and KCB Bank.[62] However, in practice, very few refugees hold bank accounts. Aspiring online freelancers will also require a refugee ID alongside other documentation to register their business with the Kenya Revenue Authority (KRA).[63]

An unexpired passport or refugee ID are further needed to register a SIM card, while other documents, such as an asylum seeker or proof of refugee registration document, are not usually accepted.[64] An official Refugee ID or Alien ID is also needed to register mobile money accounts (Alien IDs were replaced with Refugee Identity Cards when the new Refugee Act 2021 came into force). These requirements turned many refugees into digital outcasts in a country where almost everyone is using mobile money services such as

M-Pesa, which has been credited with increasing per capita consumption levels and helping to lift households out of poverty.[65] The ID-related barriers to using mobile money undermine digital livelihoods for refugees because M-Pesa can be used to withdraw money earned on platforms such as Upwork, while the digital payment service PayPal allows users in Kenya to deposit and receive money from PayPal to M-Pesa. That these barriers lock refugees out of important digital financial services is all the more disastrous because they are frequently prevented from opening bank accounts and therefore desperately need alternatives. The frequent difficulty to meet the ID requirements of these services discourages or excludes many from participating in the digital economy, while leading to new risks for others. As Abdullahi, the online freelancer in Dadaab, explained,

> The refugees don't have permanent identification. They have an alien card, and this expires every five years. Sometimes a freelancer comes in, and it might be that it is one to six months due from the date of expiry. They try to create an account, but they have a card that is about to expire. . . . If you use an alien card and it expires, they suspend your account or put the financial part of your account on hold. The same with banks: You open an account with a bank, and if the alien card expires, they call you, and even if there is money on it, they block you. It takes more than six months to a year to renew the alien card. So that's a problem.

This problem was mirrored by Fatima, who finished a course in 2019 when the organization behind the training helped her to open an account on Upwork. "I did some jobs there, only data entry. After that, my alien ID expired and my account was suspended for three months," she said during a remote interview. Being locked out of earnings from online gig work in this way poses financial risks if the returns from previous investments do not materialize as expected, as refugee online freelancers must often invest what little they have in smartphones, computers, and data.

The translator Mohamed, who was affiliated with the Dadaab Collective Freelancing Agency, equally highlighted that problems with "ID provision" can result in suspended platform accounts and an inability to withdraw money already earned. He said that verification processes often ask refugees for IDs and for an address and an apartment number, which is hardly applicable in a refugee camp such as Dadaab. Amid these challenges, it is easy for people to lose hope, he added. The challenges refugee workers faced in relation to IDs were mirrored the coordinator of a digital livelihoods program in Kenya:

> For some of the freelancers, there is also the risk of not being able to access their payment. For example, people set up their payment system, but then in the process, their identity document expires and then once the identity document expires, they are not able to get their money from the client anymore. Also, some of the clients actually just disappeared once they didn't get communications from the refugees. So, there is the underpayment that causes exploitation, there is the risk of not getting the payment and also the risk of them not getting employed at all. Some of them get trained, but then they are not able to get employed completely, because of the lack of documents to even set themselves up on the different online platforms.

The organizations working with the Dadaab Collective Freelancing Agency have worked closely with their partner Upwork to find solutions for these problems with identification and payment. Without this vital support, making an income remotely from a refugee camp would not be feasible for most beneficiaries, at least not without adopting unsafe informal workarounds.

Innovating Precarious Workarounds: Intermediaries, Fake IDs, and Proxy Accounts

In response to ID-related access restrictions, many aspiring refugee freelancers turn to precarious workarounds to access mobile connectivity and financial services. These emerging practices underline how the regulatory exclusion of refugees combines with work-related risks in the platform economy to undermine their chances to use online freelance work as a secure livelihood resource. The regulatory exclusion and problems they face at the national level translate into increased levels of precarity within the online gig economy, turning an already insecure work environment into a minefield of risks and obstacles. Those who want to access formal employment opportunities must work around regulatory restrictions by using another person's bank account or by using someone else's payment information on digital work platforms.[66] Those without valid IDs who want to register a SIM card or mobile money account may gain access through friends or family, through agents, or through a humanitarian organization with SIM cards registered to their name.[67] Others rely on their kinship networks for informal loans, or they use informal village savings and loans associations.[68] In addition to the ID-related barriers in accessing mobile connectivity and financial services, refugees who aspire to work online must adopt similar precarious workarounds if they want to open an account with a digital platform. This, in turn, leads to a range of risks.

At the workshop on digital risks in the Nairobi hotel, Peter, a refugee from South Sudan, explained that those who did not have the right ID can be forced to buy platform accounts that are registered on someone else's name. "You are using a Kenyan ID, but the photo you upload in your profile is yours. But at some point, you see yourself locked out of your profile because they manage to cross-reference this," he said, adding that this can then lead to a request by the platform for the worker to reverify their identity. If they cannot meet the request, they are locked out of their account and come under suspicion of fraud, "as a person who is impersonating," said Peter.

Another risk of using secondhand accounts and proxy IDs is exploitation by the intermediaries they come to rely on. "I used to give the broker 40 percent of my earnings to use their account ID.

That's unfair. It's a lot of money for doing nothing," said Claudine, a refugee from Rwanda who was doing online freelance work in transcription, during the discussion at the workshop in Nairobi. In some cases, using friends to receive payments for online work can also lead to unexpected outcomes, as another woman from Rwanda, Beatrice, said when talking about her experience of being exploited by an intermediary:

> There is a website that has legit work, data entry jobs, and you can't apply unless you are Kenyan. I used my friend's details and got the job. But the job was paying very good for data entry job. When I got it, the only way was to use all the information—phone number, email, ID—belonging to my friend. I told my friend the amount I will be paid, passing through her M-Pesa and forwarding to me. We agreed I give up 10 percent and get the rest. She refused to send me the money. . . . When she discovered what I will be paid, she didn't say anything. I started the job, so many small tasks, you are sitting and clicking. After one month, on Slack, we communicated there. I asked for the money, and she blocked me from the group and I never got the money. I cannot report this because it will look like she is the one who is doing the job.

The digital exclusion of refugees due to identification-related barriers translates into a range of risks that can severely disrupt their income and their livelihoods. This is especially problematic because many refugees already are in an economically vulnerable position—a vulnerability that can increase through their digital economic activities. The example above also hints at another issue: that refugees who use such informal workarounds cannot report when they are exploited, since they violated the terms of the platform. By using a fake digital identity, they do not exist as a recognized person that could contest unfair treatment through official channels. Their exclusion from the foundations of a digital economy therefore forces them to become "imposters" and "fraudsters," and a fraudster who is then defrauded is unlikely and unable to report such a crime and exploitation.

Refugees who participated in the discussions during the workshop in Nairobi talked about a vibrant market for the sale and resale of accounts on digital labor platforms. As Emmanuel, a refugee from the Democratic Republic of Congo (DRC), explained, "Someone is approved on a platform. They are approved and then they sell their account secondhand. Some good accounts can go for a lot of money. Some people keep on selling the profile." Joseph, who was also from the DRC, nodded and added, "I had a friend who wanted to start working online, had this new Upwork account, and there is such a challenge getting a job and getting paid. So, at the beginning, they can't get jobs. So, someone from outside created their account, and he lost 50.000 Kenyan Schilling [US$380] just for creating the account and doing one or two jobs, so he could get the first positive reviews."

In a similar vein, Claudine from Rwanda talked about the financial implications of buying proxy accounts, since the platforms try to stop the widespread practice and block suspicious accounts. "I made a lot of losses, so I stopped working online," she said, explaining that she no longer worked as an online freelancer. She had seen enough. "I bought four accounts, one for 25 thousand Schilling [$190] and I got locked out after around six months. Then I bought another account for 15 thousand [$114]. After a month I was locked out." Recalling how being locked out of her account prevented her from accessing some of her earnings, she said, "The last time, I almost got depressed and I thought I must stop. That account I bought with my friend for 65.000 [$500], I felt this is too much. I slept for a whole week thinking about my decision." Another former freelancer at the workshop, Miguel, also talked about his experience with account suspensions, saying that he lost around US$100. To him, the reasons behind the widespread practice among refugees was rooted in their desperation: "You just do it because you are desperate for money."

Time pressure and harmful work practices Another way in which refugees navigated the challenges of an exclusive and precarious digital economy included a harmful race against time: trying to meet deadlines despite unreliable internet connectivity and adjusting one's work schedules to bridge the gap between time zones. Some workers shared accounts so they could maximize the speed and expand the time at which they worked. "There are people sharing accounts, and some people are working with people they share the account with, they wake up at 3 a.m. . . . In this collaboration you take turns depending on time zone, or availability," said Miguel at the workshop.

The difference in time zones between the location of workers and the location of clients is difficult to bridge from a refugee camp. With electricity and internet connectivity often being restricted to certain times during the day, workers cannot easily bid for jobs that are posted in distant time zones of the United States and other major buyer countries. The pressure to resolve this temporal dissonance through hard work and informal workarounds has a negative impact on refugees' health, said Rose, a program officer with the organization RefuSHE, who used to work as a freelance transcriber in the past:

> The time difference is a problem. You get transcriptions posted while you are asleep, and that is when they are sent. So, if you want to get this work, you find yourself working under a lot of pressure [to apply for them]. This has health implications, not just physical health but also mental health. I was doing transcriptions for a while. That time issue was hard. Being exploited in terms of payment. You are checking the digital rates per hour. You are seeing that someone is paying you below minimum wage. . . . back in the days it cost me my mental stability because I needed the resources and money.

Here, the urgent need for an income combines with the precarity of platform work, which often requires a lot of unpaid labor time through constant bidding. This dynamic drives harmful work practices among refugees who can be in desperate need of an income and have limited resources. Claudine, who stopped working as an online freelancer for this reason, described the problem the following way: "There is also an issue with health in online jobs. Some of them are 24/7. After you did one and submitted, you see there are 20 dollars in your account, so you want to work more, so some people take painkillers and you have headphones on, and you keep working and get tired. You increase the volume of the audio file [when transcribing]. You don't take time to rest."

In the conversations during the workshop in Nairobi, these comments triggered many nods from others around the table, with Peter, a refugee from South Sudan, saying, "To echo what Claudine is saying, a friend of mine who was doing online work, because of time difference, I found him at 4 a.m. working and then the next day we went to class. It became an issue with his mental health, and I took him to hospital and the doctor told him you need to sleep a lot." Claudine nodded and added, "When there is a deadline, you have to submit and there is so much pressure, and when you finish, you feel sick. I didn't even have enough to eat. If I don't finish on time, my ratings are going down, and even if you are one minute late, it means you are late. People should know they should take breaks."

Adding to this precarious environment are experiences of discrimination and harassment, which are already very prevalent among Kenyan platform workers and affect refugees in particularly severe ways. Platform workers in Kenya experience discrimination based on their gender, race and ethnicity, as well as due to their location, and women are especially vulnerable and face a higher risk of online harassment and abuse.[69] All of this is in addition to their exposure to widespread scams and cybercrime.

Scamming "desperate" refugees Scammers increasingly target refugees and take advantage of their vulnerabilities, adding yet another element of risk to their insecure and challenging online work experience. As Joseph from the DRC said, there are a lot of scams targeting refugees working online, including fake job adverts on social media. "Once you click on those links, your accounts are already hacked. I had a very massive virus on my computer and had to erase everything. The tendency is to be naïve," he said. Beatrice from Rwanda added by saying that "desperation makes you click on those links," which made others around the table nod in affirmation. "That is true, desperation," Peter from South Sudan agreed, saying that one of his friends was once approached on Facebook with a scholarship offer for Canada. "She was desperate and naive and accepted the deal," he said. They asked her to transfer money to "process an ID," and the scammer mentioned various people she knew to build trust. They pretended to be organizing a visa and a flight to Canada. "They know refugees are desperate," he added. Other scams targeted them through the M-Pesa mobile money service and included fake messages about "accidental transfers" that users should refund, as well as a variety of cryptocurrency scams. Scammers also targeted refugees with resettlement scams, pretending to offer them opportunities to resettle in another country in exchange for money.

Some refugee-serving organizations have begun to increase the awareness about scams and build stronger digital resilience among beneficiaries. This includes the digital livelihoods program of the WUSC in Kenya, representatives of which attended the workshop in Nairobi. Their experience showed that "safeguarding concerns were one of the biggest deterrents to engagement with online work" among their refugee beneficiaries in Kenya.[70] Creating better awareness is seen as an important first step. As Peter from South Sudan said, "creating awareness is important, among refugees in the camp. There is desperation, and those who want to go abroad through scholarships, if they don't have the awareness, they get scammed."

This is why WUSC offers their beneficiaries a digital safeguarding module in all of their programs so they can build digital resilience.

However, it is unlikely that refugees who fall victim to cybercrime and scams will report this to the relevant authorities because they may fear that this puts them on the radar of the police or the government. As Rose from the organization RefuSHE said, refugees may fear that it could have a negative impact on their status: "If I report to the police, even if it was the police, does that make them profile me more, because of my absence of documents? If I am fully documented, and I am in the pipeline for resettlement, so if I start these legal issues, is it somehow showing up in my file? You are faced with a lot of fear. You are not fighting for your right, and yet it is your right."

Conclusion: The Bounded Opportunities and Risks of Refugee Online Work

Against the backdrop of national digital transformation, online freelance work in Kenya has become a digital extension of the country's informal labor market in which "hustling" and gig work have long been a dominant experience. This web-based digital economy has gained special significance for refugees who are confined to camps, where they face movement restrictions and a lack of suitable employment opportunities. With its abundance of jobs and virtual border-crossing potential, the transnational digital labor market comes to symbolize a source of liberation and mobility in the face of local entrapment and limitation. This liberatory potential defines the ideological underpinnings of the initiatives and programs that promote online freelance work among refugees, even if these efforts also face a myriad of barriers and challenges in realizing digital refugee livelihoods.

Some of these challenges involve barriers to access, while others result from their participation in a digital economy. With only a small minority of refugees in Kenya benefiting from digital livelihoods, the forcibly displaced remain marginalized in national digital transformation processes that ignore their specific needs and challenges. Key barriers that undermine refugees' access to a digital economy include digital skills and education, the challenges in accessing digital devices and meaningful connectivity, and ID-related barriers in registering SIM cards and opening accounts with financial service providers and digital platforms. Many challenges are rooted in a wider policy and regulatory environment that is not conducive to their digital economic inclusion. It is often in response to these exclusive policies and regulations that refugees must innovate informal and precarious workarounds that subsequently expose them to new risks.

In their efforts to circumvent the policies and regulations that exclude them, they are forced to use fake identities and false credentials as they buy used platform accounts and channel payments through the accounts of brokers and intermediaries. In fear of discrimination against freelancers who live in a refugee camp, some hide their true location from their online presence. These workarounds remain highly precarious and lead to a variety of risks, such as the financial risk of being locked out of their earnings if the platform suspends the accounts or the risk of being exploited by intermediaries who take advantage of their vulnerability and desperation. Adding their widespread exposure to scams and cybercrime only further highlights how their incorporation into a digital economy deepens existing inequalities, while also giving rise to new risks and harmful experiences.

Supported by training programs and freelancing agencies, some refugees overcome barriers and succeed as online freelancers and entrepreneurs, thereby becoming digital pioneers and role models who thrive in challenging conditions. Some of the successful pioneers have managed to create their own freelancing agencies, thereby supporting newcomers to build a reputation and earn an income through remote work. This hints at the capacity of refugees and the organizations that support them to navigate the atomization of online gig work through innovating new models of working and organizing, although such intermediation does not change the inherent insecurity and precarity of their work experience. Moreover, the majority of refugees in Kenya do not yet benefit from these initiatives. Those who do tend to be well educated, potentially leaving the most vulnerable behind.

Even for the most successful refugee online freelancers in Kenya, their work remains tightly tethered to the spatial restrictions and local conditions they face in camps. Time becomes equally restrictive and fraught with uncertainty: Amid restricted and unreliable internet connectivity in camps and the pressures of gig work, individual refugee freelancers adopt risky and harmful practices in their race against time and its restricted nature. Confined to camps with limited digital infrastructure and marginalized by a lack of financial inclusion and economic rights, many refugees in Kenya find that the ostensibly boundary-crossing digital economy is only boundary crossing in highly limited ways: The virtual mobility it enables remains bounded by the spatial, regulatory, and temporal restrictions they encounter.

All of this offers an important new perspective on what Richard Heeks calls adverse digital incorporation,[71] showing how refugees' incorporation into the platform economy converts their wider marginalization and entrapment at the national level into the transnational space of a digital economy. Within this conversion, the digital economy deepens some elements of their preexisting marginalization while forming other challenges and risks anew. As refugees experience digital livelihoods through a recurring tension between systematic exclusion and adverse incorporation, they come to inhabit an ambivalent space of digital exile, a state of being in between insecurity and entrapment on the one hand, and a powerful promise of self-reliance on the other. Against this backdrop, the refugees' experience highlights how "place, proximity, and positionality still matter" despite the hypermobility of work in digital markets at planetary scale.[72] Just like the digital economy virtually expands the space of a refugee camp, the positionality and place of a refugee online freelancer becomes imbricated with this digital economy. Promoting refugee self-reliance through the digital economy inscribes the precarity and risks of gig work into refugee livelihoods, and the restrictions and risks affecting refugees into the digital economy.

3
Coding Against All Odds

The Promises and Perils of Digital Careers for Refugees in Berlin

Aarif moved to Germany from Syria in 2013. Sitting on the terrace of a café in Berlin's *Volksgarten*, the thirty-year-old Syrian explained that he never applied for asylum because he wanted to gain social recognition through hard work. Now he was "a refugee who is not getting support as a refugee," as he put it. When the war in Syria broke out in 2011, he had just graduated with a master's degree in web technology from a local university. His parents told him not to get involved in politics. He did it anyway. Together with a friend, he managed a Facebook page that supported the "revolution" in his hometown, where he soon joined in street demonstrations. During one such protest, he was arrested and then interrogated. "I told them I don't like the instability of the revolution because I want to finish my studies," he said. All he wanted was to get things done and continue building his career, which was no longer possible in his home country. As the conflict became more violent, he felt there was increasingly little left for him to contribute, so he decided to focus on continuing his studies and his professional life elsewhere. He first moved to Turkey, from where he successfully applied for a visa to study in the German city of Magdeburg. He felt excited and ready to work hard. A few years later, when he graduated and moved to Berlin, his expectation to find a good IT job in the epicenter of the German tech scene quickly gave way to a more sobering reality. It took him a whole year and 348 job applications to get his first internship.

Aarif seemed sure that his outright rejections had something to do with his non-German name. Sometimes he even received rejection letters addressed to "Frau" (Mrs.), despite having his photograph included in the application. He said that a lot of the places he applied to must be getting thousands of applications, and when they see a "foreigner," they have a reason to reject the application. "That's one less application," he said. Aarif's perception of discrimination in this field of work is backed up by data on the European tech sector, where close to a third of workers reported discrimination based on ethnicity in one study.[1] He had to experience firsthand that the promise of inclusivity and opportunity that resonated in the German start-up scene and the IT sector was not that inclusive after all. After a long struggle, he felt lucky when he finally landed as an intern at one of Berlin's tech companies, even if it only paid the minimum wage and involved a working week of between sixty and seventy hours. Unfortunately, the internship did not lead to a real job, and he ended up unemployed once again. Not wanting to become a "welfare burden," he continued to work hard in any job he could find to sustain himself, including in a bakery and in the warehouse of a delivery service. "Maybe it would have been easier to apply for refugee status, but I didn't want any free money," he said. That his fortunes changed soon after that, when he got accepted to a traineeship position at Microsoft, was partly thanks to the support of Berlin's foremost coding school for refugees, the ReDI School of Digital Integration.

The Integrational Vision of Digital Careers

Initiatives such as the ReDI School quickly became a defining feature of Germany's response to the arrival of close to a million asylum seekers in 2015. This response saw the emergence of digital skills training and entrepreneurship programs, online platforms that offered to match refugees with jobs, and numerous hackathons that invited participants to develop tech solutions for the challenges refugees faced. The coding schools that emerged in the wake of the "refugee crisis" formed part of a broader trend of finding technological answers to the challenges of integration.[2] What was framed in terms of humanitarian aid and development among refugees hosted in the Global South was largely talked about in terms of "integration" and labor market inclusion in rich countries such as Germany.

The wider movement included actors in the field of "civic tech" or "tech for social good," which was led by motivated individuals and organizations in the tech sector that mobilized resources and efforts to innovate solutions for asylum seekers and refugees in Germany.[3] Coming from the private sector, most of these actors promoted an entrepreneurial approach to refugees' economic challenges. Digital skills training and careers in the tech sector were somewhat uncritically framed as a speedy route to self-reliance and labor market integration.[4] One underlying assumption was that highly motivated and well-educated refugees like Aarif were ready to work very hard against all odds, in part because they have little to lose and feel the pressure to prove themselves and establish a new professional life in a new country.

Berlin was at the center of refugee-supporting tech initiatives in Europe, as people from its vibrant technology and start-up sector linked their efforts to a wider "welcome culture" that defined the official German response at the time. The arrival period saw an explosion of tech-based solutions to support refugees and their socioeconomic integration. In 2016 alone, 54 out of 106 tech-related projects for refugees in Germany began in Berlin.[5] While many of these initiatives have not continued to operate permanently, some coding schools expanded to other countries and endured. Since 2015, the ReDI School has offered free training courses for refugees, migrants, and marginalized locals in a range of digital skills and other related competencies. Teaching refugees and migrants who had arrived in Germany how to write code and acquire important skills for a digitalized economy became a stepping stone for their pathways into a new professional life, and a key pillar of their wider economic and social integration in Germany.

The term "integration" is used here primarily in relation to the labor market while also reflecting discourses and dominant demands for cultural and social adaptations as part of economic inclusion. Integration in this sense forms part of the imaginary of a nation-state, including hierarchies of dominance that seek to maintain a societal status quo.[6] At the same time, we can witness a digitalization of integration pathways grounded in an imaginary that paints digital careers as a shortcut to economic inclusion both in the local economy and an international tech sector. This idea instilled powerful aspirations among refugees who knew that their positive validation as "good" refugees will be conditional on their professional success and economic contribution. The tech sector appeared to be a perfect and attractive option because of its international outlook, with a frequent possibility to get by in English. This resonated among refugees and many migrants because their entry into skilled jobs in Germany has long been made difficult by discrimination, institutionally and culturally delineated skill criteria, language requirements, and qualification requirements.[7]

The simultaneous spread of an online gig economy in Berlin and in other cities around the world offered another complementary source of income that was relatively easy to access for migrants and refugees, providing self-employed work on digital labor platforms to growing numbers of migrants who struggle to find employment elsewhere.[8] However, for most of the fairly well-educated refugees and migrants at the ReDI School, the high demand for skilled IT workers in Germany, coupled with a relatively enabling labor market policy, created realistic expectations for secure employment with the full spectrum of legally enshrined rights and benefits. Many of the middle-class refugees and migrants in Berlin considered digital skills training and coding schools because they did not qualify for other skilled work. Some of them faced difficulties in learning German language skills, even though they participated in courses. Difficulties in accrediting their preexisting qualifications posed another hurdle. They may have been doctors or lawyers in their home country, but converting their qualifications would take many years and sometimes meant having to start studying from scratch again. Becoming programmers and other IT experts was a very appealing alternative because formal degrees mattered less in the tech scene.

Digital Careers as a Shortcut to Employment and Respect

An eagerness to learn and move forward was very evident at the ReDI School's events and courses. It was a welcoming space with dedicated staff and volunteers who brought with them crucial expertise and an ability to motivate students. Cohorts of new students were usually onboarded in welcome events. One Saturday morning, I attended the kickoff event of the School's Digital Career Programme at the Microsoft Atrium event space in Berlin. From the foyer, which had large windows, a bar, and coffee tables, a door led into the main hall where staff of the ReDI School were rushing about to get the venue ready for the new students. Slowly, one after another arrived, and the spacious venue came to life with a diversity of young people, most of them refugees and migrants in their twenties and early thirties. One of the older ones among them was Hisham from Syria, whom I talked to over coffee while standing around one of the high tables in the foyer. I asked him what he hoped to get out of the program and why he wanted to start a career in the tech sector. Hisham explained that he already had a career and had worked as a lawyer in his home country before being displaced by the war in Syria. "Here, I cannot work as a lawyer because they don't accredit my degree," he explained. For him and many others who attended the event that day, digital skills and computer programming were a promising alternative: a way to establish a new kind of professional life and identity in relatively short time.

There was a strong sense of departure toward something new and exciting among the participants, many of whom were ready for a major shift in their lives and their careers. This became clear when the program manager Manuel asked the crowd of seated students what the word "onboarding" meant to them. One young man in the audience promptly answered the question by saying, "It's like we board a new plane and go to places no one has ever seen before." Manuel responded enthusiastically, saying, "Yes, it's like making a journey. You are about to take a journey today, and today is your first day. So, you are onboarded. Stay excited!" Benjamin, the director of the digital career service at the ReDI School in Berlin, later asked the participants, "Who is searching for employment here at the moment?" More than half of them put their hands up. "And who already has a job and is happy?" Only two raised their hands. It became clear that they all hoped the program would change that situation.

The aspirations of these new students of the Digital Career Programme were not unrealistic, and many had an awareness about the large number of job opportunities in Germany's technology and start-up sectors. The participants of the kickoff event I attended in February 2020 would graduate and enter the labor market at a time when, in 2021, some 96,000 jobs in Germany's IT sector remained vacant, and that number was said to increase further.[9] While the country's more traditional IT industries remained largely German speaking, Berlin was home to an international start-up scene where people from all over the world worked in open plan offices and coworking spaces, often with English as the main working language. This was one reason why the tech sector was perceived to be accessible and open to diversity. As Farid Bidarel, founder of the coding teaching initiative CodeDoor, explained, "For a migrant from Syria who used to be a teacher, there is no way that you can be a teacher here unless your German is perfect. This is just the way it is here. The same with doctors. Software developers, you can; it's an amazing potential." The ability to work in English was one of the reasons why digital skills were seen to ease and accelerate the labor market integration of well-educated refugees and migrants who already had some English language skills.

Another reason was that formal qualifications like university degrees were not necessarily a precondition for making it in the sector. The field of computer programming includes a large number of experts who taught themselves or learned through informal channels.[10] This makes coding attractive for migrants and refugees who cannot work in their former professions and therefore needed a way to launch a new career path. Many of the refugees also hoped to become coders to make up for some of the loss that forced displacement often entails: a loss of class status through the dissolution of careers and the nonrecognition of qualifications.[11] In this sense, becoming computer programmers and other digitally skilled specialists resembled both an acceleration and a leapfrogging opportunity, a step up and a thrust forward: It resembled a chance to reinstate a certain economic status, and it offered a shortcut to employment and to remaking one's professional identity. When students at the ReDI School were asked what they wanted to get out of the course at an event, they all replied "respect," said Sarya, a JavaScript student. "This is because no one respects us. We feel like cockroaches here." The hope for gaining "respect" through work in the IT sector represented an opportunity to overcome an enduring sense of outsiderness and degradation that many refugees experienced.

No Desire for Gig Work

The aspirations of Syrian refugees in Germany's digital skills training programs were somewhat surprising to me early on in my research. Based on its significance in other refugee-hosting regions, such as the Middle East and East Africa, I had come to Berlin with the idea that online freelancing is likely going to be widespread among young skilled refugees who struggled to find local employment. However, the most frequent response I received from coding school students and other well-educated refugees in Berlin was that they did not aspire to work as online freelancers at all. They were working toward a proper well-paid job, the availability of which was evidenced by data on the high number of vacant IT positions.

Those who worked as online freelancers often did so only to complement their income while studying, or as a side hustle. Platform work was sometimes a necessity but never engendered the kind of aspiration it did among refugees in Kenya or Lebanon, where local employment opportunities were highly restricted and refugees faced many other spatial, legal, and regulatory limitations. One of the remote freelance opportunities for refugees in Germany was with NaTakallam (Arabic for "we speak"), the social enterprise offering language services and remote language tutoring provided by refugees and other conflict-affected people. One of their language trainers was Salah, whom I first met in a remote interview in spring 2019. Salah first went to Istanbul from Syria but soon decided to make his way toward Europe via Greece. He told me about his difficult crossing, with their boat coming close to sinking and an emergency evacuation to the Moria camp in Greece. After a month or so in the camp, he heard about some of the European borders being closed and decided to continue his journey, walking all the way to Athens together with large numbers of other refugees. "We were fifteen people in Athens and lived on the streets. We heard about empty houses and started to squat, cleaning the place and making it our own," he said. He was one of few who spoke good English, which helped him to get a job with an NGO while working on his resettlement application with the United Nations. He eventually came to Germany in 2017.

When we first talked over Skype, which was the preferred platform used by NaTakallam at the time, Salah had already done ten months of German language courses and tried to develop his programming skills independently online. His work with NaTakallam was a welcome side income, but he was worried about doing more self-employed online work, saying, "I am trying to learn more about freelancing . . . but you don't have insurance, and I am not sure how to find a way to turn that into a career. Sometimes you work seven hours a day, but the pay is not that good." To be sure, working through initiatives like NaTakallam helped him to make extra money, although "that money does not help me to build my future," he explained, saying, "It's just some extra money, like you do work on the side." Working as a remote freelancer will not help him integrate into the German economy either, he added. However, he found that doing such online work involves less exposure to discrimination than searching for employment on the ground.

The young Syrian Anas also gave me the impression that freelancing was not a viable aspiration for well-educated refugees in Berlin. I met him on the terrace of a café on Berlin's *Alexanderplatz*. Similar to Aarif, who was introduced earlier, Anas insisted that he was "not a refugee," saying, "I didn't apply for refugee status because I feel that would be lazy. It would make me be lazy." He left Syria for Erbil, the capital of Iraq's Kurdish region, where he worked in the IT sector until political developments led to an exodus of tech companies. "After that, I realized I had to go to another country, but as a Syrian, I didn't have too many options, so I went to Malaysia. I took a flight to Kuala Lumpur and tried my luck." A ninety-day tourist visa was enough for him to find a job as a back-end developer working on several shorter projects, even if "the work was bad," as he explained. He had left Malaysia for Germany about a year before we met. His brother was already in Berlin, and so he decided to apply for a job-seeker visa, which he eventually got. He said that his arrival in Berlin "was a new chapter" in his life. When we spoke, I asked him if he ever considered working as an online freelancer. He shook his head and said it wasn't really for him. After all, he had enough experience to find a "proper job" in Germany. His journey to such a proper job was not that straightforward, however. He soon left a first job as a back-end developer because it was isolating and lacked mentorship and support. The job search that followed took about four months. Just when he was ready to apply for asylum because he ran out of options, he finally found a new job that met his expectations.

Syrian refugees in Berlin also found that online freelancing was not really what most people from their country would consider to be an acceptable and proper job, indicating how cultural and social factors influence its adoption. Being a freelancer did not involve the kind of "respect" a proper job did. It was also too insecure for many to be a real consideration. As the developer and author Akram explained when we met in Berlin, "Online freelancing, if I'd think what is required for online freelancing: its flexibility and some level of security. How many refugees really have that?" He added that "this kind of freelancing economy does not exist in any of our hometowns in Syria, at least not when I still lived there. You have employees, and entrepreneurs." Online freelancing tends to be a rather insecure form of self-employment that takes place in a global digital labor market that is detached from local society and people. This made it less desirable for well-educated refugees in Berlin. After all, the city had plenty of relevant jobs in digital fields of work, and Syrian refugees enjoyed the right to work and had access to a wide range of support mechanisms.

They felt that with enough hard work and sufficient motivation, they could become employees in a new profession very soon.

"The Industry Needs People Who Are Hungry"

The tendency among the young Syrians I met in Berlin to reject the label of "refugees" and emphasize their willingness to work hard mirrored the demand for dedication and hard work in coding circles: The idea was that everyone can become a coder as long as they are motivated, hardworking, and willing to make sacrifices. Wael from Syria came to Germany at the later stages of his degree in archaeology and found work after several courses at the ReDI School. When asked whether he thought anyone can be successful as a coder, he said, "Not really if you don't really like it. . . . A lot of people should have the chance to get to know the field. Only the ones who love it should stay in this field." This somewhat mirrored the "do what you love" mantra in creative digital economies, where powerful appeals to passion and entrepreneurialism are mobilized toward a desired future goal, and all investments and sacrifices are expected to pay off and increase one's status: a kind of "aspirational labor" and a "romance with work."[12]

The volunteers and beneficiaries in digital skills training courses often seemed to invoke such an approach, framing hard work as fun and coding as passion. In a beginner JavaScript class at the ReDI School, the teacher Nadia embodied such enthusiasm about the challenges of coding. After she went through some of the first tasks of the course with the students, an error popped up. She then turned to the class, saying, "When the code turns red, I always get excited because I love debugging code!" This enthusiasm was highly encouraged among students in classes and at career workshops. During an online meeting of the ReDI School, which was part of a series of events titled "A Day in the Life of . . . ," a software developer and volunteer mentor offered descriptions of his job and gave tips while repeating how the enthusiasm and eagerness of refugee students at the school was their core appeal to employers. "Your weakness—your lack of experience—is also your strength. You come with fresh eyes, and a hunger. You come and want to find a job. Many of us get comfortable. We have a job and we get lazy. The industry needs people who are hungry."

This also played at the idea that refugees who have suffered the tribulations of displacement and endured the cumbersome bureaucracy of the immigration regime will be willing to work hard. They are eager to uplift themselves from their marginal position in the German economy. In order words, they were understood to be particularly well suited for the rapid learning, adjustment, and commitment demanded by the IT sector because of their experience of migration and displacement. The Syrian woman Hanan from Syria invoked a similar sense of hardiness. She came to Germany in 2018 and hoped to find a job in the insurance industry where she had worked for some years in her hometown. She felt that her experience as a Syrian prepared her well for this. "Syrians are used to transformations," she said. "If someone says this is very complicated and you will need two months to complete it, I will get it done in one month." Although Hanan came to Germany on a student visa, she articulated how her Syrian-ness and experience of war and hardship made her particularly well suited to becoming a coder. Young refugees and migrants like Hanan were considered to be the ideal subjects for a process of remaking newcomers into hardworking coders with an entrepreneurial spirit. Digital skills were promoted as the tools they needed to succeed in that process of remaking.

This remaking of refugees and migrants into skilled specialists for the tech sector represents a promising path to their economic integration and success. Viewed together, the many individual pathways of people who succeeded in the tech sector became icons of how technological innovation and national policies of integration can work together, while also symbolizing the transformative potential of an international tech-driven city.

Refugee Coders and the German Immigration Regime

The German government has promoted migrants and asylum seekers to be entrepreneurial and self-sufficient in a myriad of ways, symbolized not least in the German Chancellor Angela Merkel's visit to the ReDI School in Berlin in 2017. After all, professional success is seen as the antidote to refugees as a "public burden," which is exemplified by the frequent refusal to apply for asylum among highly skilled forcibly displaced people who came to Germany on student visas or found employment. Becoming a coder was one way of preventing long-term dependence on social benefits while also making refugees and migrants contribute economically to meet skills shortages in certain sectors.[13] Digital skills training institutions become important actors that help achieve this dual aim of increasing refugee employment and filling skills shortages in the technology sector.

The inclusive promise of a tech sector and the support of coding schools combine to suggest a leapfrogging opportunity for skilled refugees and migrants who would otherwise face significant obstacles in accessing skilled employment. Germany has a well-protected skilled labor market that is defined by a dual education system that combines apprenticeships with vocational training. One survey by the German Job Agency found that 68 percent of refugees in Germany want to learn a new profession or enter higher education.[14] But partly because of concerns over immigrants' potential role in devaluing German qualifications and professions if requirements were eased, migrants and refugees faced a lot of difficulties in accessing apprenticeships.[15]

A Skilled Immigration Act, which was first widely discussed in 2020, promised to open more professions to people with tertiary education and those who can prove professional training that is *equivalent* to a German degree, including those acquired in the dual education system.[16] The act, which was passed by parliament in June 2023, has three pillars. First, it aimed to offer easier access to residence permits for "skilled workers" whose qualifications or degrees were either obtained in Germany or are considered equivalent. Second, it also allowed skilled workers with no accepted equivalent qualification to work in Germany if they have appropriate work experience of at least two years, have a minimum salary, and have completed an apprenticeship that is formally accepted by the home country and took at least two years (the foreign degree does not have to be recognized as equivalent). The third pillar focuses on "potential" and offers a so-called "chance card" with a temporary residence permit and access to the labor market for those without a job offer who have certain prequalifications and language skills and show potential due to their specific skills and are looking for employment or possibilities to get their foreign vocational qualifications recognized as equivalent.[17] Although initial drafts of the law suggested that those who would be eligible for a skilled worker's visa but already lived in Germany cannot apply, this has been relaxed in a later revision, potentially making digital skills training programs key instruments for refugees and migrants to obtain residency.

In this sense, coding schools filled an important gap in the German immigration regime because they turned refugees and migrants who were already in the country into skilled specialists. This aligned well with national strategies while also responding to the needs of the tech sector and the international tech-driven city of Berlin. The city's often-cited openness toward diversity and immigration also aids a steady inflow of international workers with important skills. Berlin has long had the highest share of immigrants and migrants in the population among Germany's regions.[18] Although cities are dependent on national migration regimes, they often implicitly pursue immigration strategies in a proactive and open-minded manner to reduce the financial and social costs of their presence.[19] Berlin historically had high unemployment rates up to a peak of 19 percent in 2005, which was before it officially established itself as a tech-driven economy and a multicultural city.[20] The ReDI School and other related initiatives have shown that there is significant skill potential among refugees already in the country, who are in fact skilled migrants "in progress" who will ultimately fill gaps in the labor market. However, highly skilled jobs in IT are not representative of the wider refugee population, considering that some 210,000 refugees and asylum seekers were registered as unemployed with the job agency in 2020.[21] In mid-2024, already over 426,000 forcibly displaced people were unemployed in Germany.[22]

With rising numbers of unemployment and labor market competition often come tensions between refugees and host communities. Yet even the experience of highly skilled foreign IT specialists in urban economies is not immune to inequalities and racism. Digital capitalism and the establishment of global high-tech hubs has long built on migrants and IT specialists from the Global South, who often faced precarious employment conditions and insecure legal statuses.[23] Berlin, too, has pulled IT experts from India and other non-white migrant workers into its international digital economy, where they often worked in short-term employment without secure residency. This incorporation often involved a contradictory experience for skilled migrants in the IT sector, who are middle-class professionals with high career aspirations but also experience discrimination and racism within the wider German immigration regime.[24] At heart, the contradiction that aspiring refugee IT workers in Berlin and other cities experience is one between promises of social mobility for *anyone* in the tech sector, which instill a universally accessible "vision of success," and an individual experience that involves frequent reminders that migrant and refugee "others" are, in fact, not an equal part of this "universal" vision.[25] For refugees in particular, learning how to code may offer access to a seemingly universally recognized skill set that unlocks a pathway to formal employment, but it also represents one way of trying to qualify as a "good" refugee that is deserving of integration and access to a job.[26]

Labor market access of refugees and other migrants in Germany is governed by a nonpermanent German residence permit.[27] Every migrant, asylum seeker, or refugee with a residence permit who lacks German language skills must attend an integration course, while some laws and policies, like the 2016 Integration Bill, apply to asylum seekers and refugees specifically.[28] Overall, the integration regime is designed to punish those who become a "public burden" while rewarding those who contribute: If a refugee welfare recipient failed to take part in the labor market or work scheme, social benefits could be cut and their settlement permit could be withheld, while those who succeeded in acquiring advanced German skills and securing their own livelihood were rewarded with the prospect of permanent settlement after three years. Many of the refugee coding students will therefore have faced the double pressure of learning how to code and becoming well "integrated" while learning German.

Building the Right Mindset: Why Not Everyone Can Become a Coder

There is a certain tension between the idea that everyone can become a coder and the specific expectations of what qualities and capabilities that person requires to succeed. Coding schools teach in-demand technical skills, but the road to success for refugees is also said to require a more fundamental process of adaptation: The demand for "soft skills" suggests a need for sociocultural adaptation, not only referring to nontechnical competencies like communication skills but also indirectly referring to character traits and a "culture fit" that has specific implications for some migrants and refugees. They find themselves confronted with a self-consciously cosmopolitan tech scene that has its own sociocultural norms. Digital integration therefore requires not only the mastering of digital skills but also the understanding and "decoding" of the IT sector's working culture, in addition to the wider social demands for integration and cultural assimilation and pressures to master national integration policies and bureaucracies.

This is similar to how digital skills and livelihood programs in countries such as Kenya and Lebanon encourage refugees to adopt a different mindset, which includes a need to think in entrepreneurial ways while accepting risks and insecurity in exchange for access to new markets. Although a digital economy has accelerated and reshaped this process into new forms, it is embedded in a longer shift away from placing refugees into formal work toward promoting more insecure and informal work through livelihoods training and entrepreneurship.[29] Organizations that run these programs have been actively involved in attempts to reshape refugees' mentality away from one that prioritizes security and relies on aid toward one more closely aligned with the idea of self-reliance and entrepreneurship.[30] What has been discussed less frequently is how this process intersects with requirements of a "good" and self-reliant refugee who must adapt to both the national majority culture and the specific working culture of a digital economy. In this sense, the dual need of learning to code and decoding the working culture of tech companies in Berlin mirrors official demands for cultural integration and being a self-sufficient and economically contributing immigrant. This is very different from the incorporation of refugees into online gig work in countries with highly restrictive refugee regimes and encampment policies, where online freelance work becomes an escape route from the lack of local and national integration rather than one of its foundations. Succeeding in tech among refugees in Germany, however, becomes a continuation of integrational efforts by digital means.

This raises the question about how many refugees actually succeeded. The Digital Career Programme at the ReDI School built in-demand skills, but its relatively short program, often only with four hours of training a week, was not always enough to get a good job. The head of the program estimated in a conversation that each year only around 10 to 20 percent of students on the intermediate program go on to get an internship or job soon after they graduate. A survey designed together with the ReDI School offers a more detailed insight about job placement after trainings: Refugees generally had lower full-time employment rates than non-refugees, while more time passed since graduation among students meant higher chances of employment.

Overall, 40 percent of the 101 graduates we surveyed in autumn 2020 stated they were working full time, 20 percent were not working, 8 percent worked part time, and 5 percent did an internship (the "other" category included freelancers, entrepreneurs, or students). This data included those who graduated from ReDI courses between 2016 and 2019, but if we look at those thirty-seven graduates who had finished their last course most recently, in 2019, the share of those who worked full time fell to 35 percent, suggesting that more time is crucial for success in finding a decent job. Among the fifty-one respondents that declared their refugee status, the share of those working full time was only 29 percent, compared to the 40 percent overall, while 25 percent of refugees stated they were not working at all. A closer look at graduates' jobs shows that many of those who found employment or traineeships worked in highly skilled digital fields, including as software programmers, web developers, data scientists, or engineers. However, some appeared to work in largely unrelated fields, including as "receptionist," "social worker," "shop assistant," or "delivery driver."

The need to speak German was cited as a major barrier in accessing employment by about 32 percent of the surveyed graduates overall, and by 38 percent of the respondents who were refugees. At the same time, excellent English skills are needed too and have been lacking among many of the Syrian refugees who moved to

Germany. This is why many programs and initiatives that focused on creating tech jobs for refugees primarily targeted those whom the developer and author Akram called "an elite group of refugees," saying, "digital integration does not work for all refugees. In fact, by doing it, you already eliminate a lot of refugees."

Akram had studied IT for four years in Syria but did not work in anything tech-related until he came to Berlin. He wanted to go back to university but realized that he would need to learn German at a very high level to do that, saying that "learning a language intensively for two years was not really what I felt like. Then, I thought, why don't I study coding myself?" With the help of a coding initiative, he was able to upskill quickly and managed to find decent employment in a field he liked. Many others, however, struggled to find the necessary motivation, time, and competencies that were needed in addition to the technical skills. One of the reasons why many students did not make it into the well-paid jobs in local startups and IT companies may have been their difficulty to develop key skills that are not technical at all.

Anne Kjaer-Riechert, the founder of ReDI School, told the audience at her TEDx talk in 2017,[31] as she showed a picture of crowded tables at one of the first classes of ReDI School in 2016, "You will notice from that picture there is not a computer in sight. [This is] because we believe that learning to code is not just about the ability to write beautiful code. It's about developing a problem-solving mindset to come up with . . . solutions for society." Problem-solving is not the only part of the "mindset" that coding schools for migrants and refugees around the world promote—this mindset may also require a willingness to work for low or no pay, the readiness to build one's reputation through internships or unpaid work. Not unlike self-employed platform workers in Kenya's refugee camps, who invest days of un- and underpaid labor to acquire gigs and build a reputation, similar sacrifices were also built into the formal digital career pathways of refugees in Berlin.

The need to build the right mindset included the demand for developing the right soft skills. The meaning of "soft skills" can be stretched to cover a range of skills, attributes, and traits. In digital skills training for refugees, soft skills further encompass "interpersonal 'people' skills as well as character traits."[32] Refugees who take part in digital skills training courses must change themselves before they can change their career, which requires them to hide certain aspects of who they are while making other traits more visible. Aimee, the head of a novice training program at Babbel, a language learning platform, saw soft skills as a form of "culture fit" in an international tech scene. This "culture" was unlike the need to fit into a specific German work culture because of a diversity of backgrounds among staff and the company's global reach: "Babbel is a very cool place to work. We have over fifty-eight nationalities," she explained. Aimee further defined "culture fit" to include a strong sense of initiative and developing "a learning culture," which she related specifically to Babbel's mission of driving language learning. Coding schools mirrored this need for a learning culture, "to teach how to learn coding, rather than provide the actual resources themselves," according to Farid, the founder of CodeDoor. Continuous self-improvement becomes part of the required mindset.

Soft skills also referred to an ability to fit in and perform expected behavioral norms, which can put assimilative pressures on the diverse backgrounds of migrants and refugees that mirror some of the demands in the national integration regime. This becomes clear in a story told by Bassem, a Sudanese master's student studying at ReDI School, about a Pakistani friend who was one of two people left for a job at a major multinational IT company. After getting through what Bassem described as "twenty interviews," and despite having all the same skills and qualifications, his friend did not get the job. According to him, the company justified this by saying that he did not look "friendly" enough. The demand for soft skills can become a euphemism for not being "friendly," or perhaps not culturally familiar enough—or, in some instances, not being white or male enough.

Tech culture is often described as being oriented around "a young white man who's single."[33] Berlin's Meetup scene, which normally consists of "pizza and beer" evenings held in the open-plan offices or foyers of companies, exemplifies this culture. These spaces are inclusive because anyone who signs up can attend, but their standard format also presents a number of informal barriers. Nakeema, the head of FrauenLoop, a coding school focused on women, considered Meetups to be exclusionary to a range of people, including, for example, some Middle Eastern women. In her opinion, there is a risk with Meetups: "It's not welcoming, it's not safe necessarily, it's not accommodating to different lifestyles." While the tech scene offers opportunities to circumvent some of the strictures of the German labor market, it demands complicated processes of change and adaptation from refugees. To what extent, then, does the IT sector's promise of a shortcut to decent work reflect the experiences of refugees and migrants who study at coding schools and search for work?

Digital Careers as a Shortcut Full of Obstacles

The hopeful aspirations of students at the ReDI School were often met by a more sobering reality in the process of applying for jobs and looking for work. In regular career counseling sessions, the beneficiaries of the school had access to support, which often included a process of balancing their aspirations with the reality of the labor market. There were plenty of examples of refugees who made it in the IT sector among volunteer teachers at ReDI School and in the wider community. Some of this was apparent in posts shared on the school's Slack channel, where announcements frequently celebrated when someone was hired by a company. Many students had the expectation that learning to code could offer what it appeared to promise: access to employment in ways that diverged considerably from other sectors in the labor market, which had more formal and conservative requirements. Few, however, considered finding a junior role or traineeship as a developer to be easy. As Manuel of the ReDI School explained, for every instance of someone who is successful, there are people who can spend two to three years searching for a job without success: "It is not only what you know, but who you are, and luck, and self-esteem." For the majority of people, coding as a shortcut to decent work was an uncertain, stilted, and bumpy journey.

"It Gets Very Muddy"

Something was not right among the approximately thirty students who attended the "Start Your Tech Career" workshop at ReDI School led by Fabienne, an HR specialist serving the IT sector in Berlin. The workshop was an upbeat introduction to the sector with the presentation outlining the many jobs available and explaining why Berlin is the best place to access them. "If you can't make it in Berlin, you can't make it anywhere. Berlin is the tech hub in Germany," she said, adding that one way of getting your foot in the door was to go to networking events and meetups. She attended three of these meetups a week. "Berlin is a village," she said. And it is "a city where you don't need to speak German," and you "don't need a fancy degree. You need experience." These words epitomize the idea that the tech sector of Berlin offers a shortcut to employment that circumvents some of the barriers and bureaucracy of other sectors in the economy.

As the event continued, there was apparent tension between the optimism of the charismatic presenter and the lived experience of many of the students. Midway through the presentation, one or two students quietly gathered their things and shuffled out of the cavernous main office at ReDI School. Well into the Q&A and with half the attendees no longer present, the problem was framed eloquently by one student, a migrant from Africa in his early thirties. Gesturing to what he understood as the subtext of the doubts being shared, he explained, "It gets very muddy. All I see [in job adverts] is CSS, JavaScript, UX design; it's pretty high. Even traineeships, there is a long list. You look at the list and you just have one line [of the criteria you meet]." There was general agreement from the rest of the class. Some 30 percent of surveyed ReDI alumni agreed that one of the main barriers they faced in finding a good job with the skills they learned was that "the jobs I want require too many skills I don't have."

Alongside these high demands by employers, the students expressed concern about discrimination. As a black woman in the class asked Fabienne, "Is it really necessary to include a picture on a CV and risk being discriminated against?" It was a question that echoed the concerns of many job seekers. Tahir, another ReDI School student from Syria, experienced that being a foreigner determined the challenges he faced in applying for jobs: "Most people don't want to employ you unless you've worked here before; maybe because of the language, or they had a bad experience with foreigners." Indeed, some 36 percent of ReDI alumni we surveyed found that the "need to have gained work experience in Germany" posed a major barrier, which rose to 43 percent among those with refugee status. The frequent demand for local work experience for Tahir was an expression of the risk employers associated with employing "foreigners." Requirements for "national" job experience are widespread in Germany and beyond, as demands for national work experience in skilled job adverts serve as a means of differentiating between natives and immigrants.[34]

Hopes of a shortcut to decent jobs in the IT sector often did not materialize, as refugees and migrants confronted the high demands of employers as well as discrimination. Progress was also full of false starts, and finding a decent job as a programmer and software developer could take several years after completion of the coding school trainings, if it materialized at all. Part of these long journeys were often episodes of working in precarious conditions in low-paid jobs and internships that the students saw as a chance to gain a foot in the door of tech companies. One common example was part-time, minimum wage work as content moderators through third-party providers for social media companies such as Facebook.

Working for long hours to survive economically and avoid becoming a welfare "burden" made it difficult to invest the passion and total commitment needed for success. Salim, a Syrian man who was in his early thirties and had studied law before coming to Germany in 2015, took on a "part-time" job at Amazon, thinking this would bring him much-needed income while also leaving him with half his time to learn how to write code at the ReDI School. However, the job entailed several hours of unpaid overtime on a regular basis, and a few weeks into work, Salim found that it created new challenges. When he could attend coding classes, he was tired and unfocused. Far from a smooth and rapid transition to a new world of work, Salim's aspirations to become a coder led him to confront the familiar slog of low-paid and undervalued work among migrants and refugees.

Precarious working conditions were a reality for many of the highly skilled refugees and migrants who looked for jobs in the IT sector. Some graduates who did internships felt they were being exploited by their employers, as was the case for Wael from Syria: A year after graduating from the ReDI School, he got an internship with a digital advertising firm but soon saw himself working seven months without any pay, despite having been an integral part of the company's website development team. "It's hard to be in a place where you are not getting paid at all," he said. When he did eventually manage to negotiate his pay, it was lower than average, but "it was my only option," he explained. His disappointment with pay turned into growing frustration after he got married, saying that "what I'm making is not enough, it was never enough, but I accepted it because I was building a career."

Un- or underpaid internships are certainly not specific to digital careers in Berlin, nor are they unique to the experience of migrants and refugees. Nonetheless, their experience underlines how migrants and refugees, who are in a hurry to rebuild their careers in a new host country, may be especially vulnerable to exploitation through internships and other unpaid roles, which can turn into a form of "aspirational labour" where sacrifices and exploitative conditions are tolerated because they are all seen to lead to an aspired goal in the future.[35] Refugees' vulnerability to such aspirational labor and its potential for exploitation are inherently connected to their status as forcibly displaced people who are expected, and often expect themselves, to prove their "worth" through hard work and success in the new society and economy.

Continuing Uncertainty Despite Success

The experience among refugees in Germany and its labor market was fraught with uncertainties and insecurities, partly driven by experiences of discrimination. Aarif's difficult early work experiences led him to conclude that Germany's attitude toward newcomers was that "you are here to do certain kinds of jobs." One of Aarif's internships in Berlin involved a racist colleague and working sixty- to seventy-hour weeks while being paid just over eight Euros an hour, hoping to prove himself so he may get a chance to transform the internship into a full-time contract. In the end, this didn't happen. After the internship, Aarif struggled to support himself but actively resisted help from the Jobcentre because he did not want to become a "welfare burden," which was also part of the reason why he never applied for asylum and moved on to support himself through work in a warehouse. Around this time, his fortune changed, however: Volunteering at the ReDI School gave him access to a good network, and one of his colleagues introduced him to Cisco, the multinational technology company, which helped him to get noticed in his application. "It wasn't special treatment, but it did mean I didn't get an automatic red line from an online bot," he explained, referring to the use of algorithms to select candidates for job posts. In this "algorithmic game," international applicants can be far less likely than German applicants to be selected due to inbuilt biases.[36] Not only was he successful at Cisco, but he also turned this job down because he made it into the highly competitive traineeship program at Microsoft. "If we had spoken a month ago, I would have given you a very different picture," he explained when we met.

Soon his great achievement was once again overshadowed by uncertainty: In late March 2020, he received a letter from the Foreigners' Office explaining that he must leave the country because of overstaying his student visa. His current "training contract" with Microsoft did not earn above the threshold required to remain. The decision did not seem to consider his secured place on the graduate scheme with Microsoft that started in autumn of the same year. A lawyer told Aarif that this might simply be a "technical issue" that could be cleared up when he started his well-paid role in September, which is eventually what happened. But for Aarif, the experience was much more than a technical mistake. The letter had come at a time when years of learning and hard work finally paid off and he made it into a program with one of the world's leading technology companies. The experience spoke of an enduring vulnerability and outsiderness and renewed the uncertainty refugees often have about their rights and legal status. The letter momentarily destabilized the idea that professional success and recognition as a "good refugee" would lead to permanent integration. In saying, "I'm not a refugee. I'm not asking for help," he once again underlined his self-sufficiency and autonomy, invoking his adherence to a regime of conditional inclusion in which "good" immigrants are those who work hard to deserve it.[37] Aarif perceived the letter as an expression of total disregard for his well-being, "as someone they are sending back to a warzone at the time of a pandemic."

Conclusion: Coding Schools and the Digital Integration of Refugees

"Learning programming is similar to learning a language. As long as you have the mental capacity, you just need time. The idea is that you just take any refugee for several months into a coding program and then, bang! It's done. But he won't be ready for the job."

This statement by the Berlin-based developer and author Akram encapsulates the powerful idea that coding schools offer a shortcut to employment for refugees that is not always met by the corresponding reality on the ground. The journeys of refugees who participate in digital skills training in Berlin are full of opportunities, and some of them lead to formal employment in a digital field of work. Yet, these journeys are also fraught with uncertainties and difficulties in adapting not only to the labor market of a new country but also to a new world of digital work. By training refugees in digital skills that are in high demand in the German labor market, coding schools play a crucial role in producing the kind of skilled "immigrants" that the country's integration policies aspire to attract. The high hopes of refugees are fueled by the powerful promise that anyone who works hard can succeed as a coder, that IT specialists are needed, and that the international tech sector allows them to circumvent some of the barriers that slow their access to the German labor market at large.

As coding students begin to apply for jobs and evaluate their career options, they often realize that the shortcut they have chosen is not that short after all. The ostensibly inclusive, nondiscriminatory, and diverse tech sector emerges as highly competitive and comes with its own demands for passionate, totally committed, and "culturally fitting" candidates. Unpaid or underpaid internships and short-term work are widespread and often add to the workload of refugees who struggle to make ends meet while simultaneously attending mandatory language and integration courses. As forcibly displaced people who face a myriad of barriers to meaningful employment, refugees are particularly susceptible to the powerful promise of digital careers to be fast, inclusive, and international, not least because they are often unable to accredit preexisting qualifications in the host country. Especially for middle-class refugees who have not only lost a homeland but also a professional identity and class status, the accelerated social mobility that the digital economy promises symbolizes a way out of being a "refugee" in need of aid to becoming a skilled "good" immigrant that contributes to the economy.

In this sense, coding schools come to fulfill several key functions within the wider German integration regime and for the tech-driven economy of Berlin. Their efforts mirror government strategies that call for entrepreneurial and self-sufficient skilled migrants that contribute economically and fill gaps in the labor market. In utilizing the tech sector's inclusive potential for non-German speakers and for specialists without formal degrees, coding schools are able to bypass some barriers of the German labor market while simultaneously fulfilling key aims of national employment policies: driving economic integration by teaching skills that are needed in the labor market and driving sociocultural integration by showing graduates how to fit into a key sector of the economy "culturally." Not only must migrants and refugees prove their integrative efforts, but they must also adapt to the specific characteristics and working culture of the international technology sector of Berlin. It follows that such "integration" becomes both national and international, requires speaking German and English, and demands extraordinary dedication and a willingness to work hard.

Considering the case of refugee coding school participants in Berlin against the backdrop of a wider digital economy in the context of forced displacement paints a very different picture than that of major refugee-hosting countries in the Global South. The high demand for skilled IT workers in the "start-up capital" of one of the world's largest economies, combined with refugees' unrestricted right to work, shifts the focus away from online and remote work to formal employment in local digital jobs. In this context, online freelancing may serve as a useful side hustle and a welcome source of additional income, but it rarely inspires the level of investment and motivation that can be found among refugees living in low- and middle-income countries such as Kenya or in those affected by severe economic crises, such as Lebanon. While digital skills training in Germany is being framed as a pathway to integration and recognition within the host country, digital skills training for refugees in highly restrictive and challenging contexts, such as Kenya and Lebanon, are primarily seen as a potential way to circumvent local restrictions and overcome the limitations of the local economy and its lack of employment opportunities for refugees.

4
Exiled in the Digital Economy

Visions of Liberation and Risk in the Hypermobile Refugee Ghetto

The introduction to this book situated the emergence of digital refugee livelihoods in the confluence of two major global trends: the unprecedented needs resulting from a consistent rise of forced displacement for over a decade and the rapid expansion of a digital economy and new forms of digital and remote work around the world. Although the promotion of digital skills and digital jobs among refugees has continued to spread despite changing political and economic environments, current and future transformations in displacement and in digitalization will inevitably reshape both the opportunities and challenges that are involved. Globally, some 123 million were forcibly displaced by 2025, and some 37 million of them were registered refugees. Each of Syria, Venezuela, Ukraine, and Afghanistan alone had over 6 million of its people living as refugees abroad.[1] Hardly a year passes without news of yet another major forced displacement crisis. As conflicts and disasters uproot more people who become tomorrow's new refugees, others may soon return home or face deportation. Some may even become permanent residents or citizens of their host countries. Yet others will remain in limbo for years or decades to come.

The magnitude of human suffering involved in the conflicts and disasters that cause displacement remains difficult to grasp. Violent conflict in Sudan forced some 11.3 million people from their homes and displaced 3 million people into neighboring countries, creating what the UN termed a dire humanitarian crisis of "epic proportions."[2] Ninety percent of Gaza's 2.1 million population were internally displaced by Israeli warfare and its conflict with Hamas, with over 50,144 Palestinians killed by spring 2025.[3] The displaced lacked access to sufficient shelter, food, life-saving medical services, clean water, education, and livelihoods.[4] As the conflict soon spread into Lebanon, it involved cross-border strikes between Hezbollah and Israel, which assassinated the group's leadership and carried out a ground invasion, all of which further eroded the country's economy and its digital infrastructures. In Syria, the Assad regime fell in December 2024 after over fifty years of dictatorship, following a sustained military campaign by opposition forces. This prompted many governments of refugee-hosting countries to halt Syrian asylum applications and start thinking about voluntary and forced returns, even as the situation on the ground remained very volatile.

Rapid technological changes and the impact of AI on the digital economy create an equally volatile environment. One study found that the number of posts for automation-prone online freelancing jobs related to writing and coding decreased by 21 percent in only eight months of ChatGPT's emergence, increasing competition over fewer and increasingly complex jobs.[5] Social enterprises that promote jobs in the field of data annotation among refugees, a type of work that trained AI through manual labor, worry that the advance of AI would soon make the most basic tasks their refugee workers are trained in obsolete or more complex. This will likely further the already strong polarization of skills in online work, with many jobs involving more complex and higher-paid tasks alongside those involving low-paid microtasks. Even on microtask platforms and many other forms of gig work, the levels of education and competition are generally very high.[6]

At the same time, scandals around the conditions of digital workers have surfaced in many places, not least in Kenya, where the death of a Nigerian content moderator who worked for a subcontractor of TikTok fueled outrage over precarious working conditions, such as low pay, lack of mental health support, long working hours, intimidation, and exposure to harmful content. This was after more than one hundred former Facebook content moderators sued the social media company over "horrible working conditions."[7]

Some of these developments cast doubt on the suitability and feasibility of digital jobs for refugees at a larger scale and demand rapid adaptation from refugee workers and from the initiatives that support them. Rising humanitarian needs and persistent development challenges, and major cuts in aid funding, including a radical reduction of US foreign development assistance in 2025, severely impacted the long-term sustainability of digital livelihood initiatives that support refugees. The increasing demand for highly skilled and more complex digital work threatened to leave refugees even farther behind, with demand-driven training programs becoming more time intensive, more costly, and possibly also more selective about beneficiaries by prioritizing those with higher skill levels who promise a higher likelihood of positive outcomes. The already crucial role of the private sector in digital livelihoods programs has been growing further as widening gaps in public aid funding emerged.

Drawing wider comparative insights from research in such a rapidly evolving field across vastly different contexts is certainly a challenging task, but also one that can offer important insights about the underlying trends and continuities that shape the intersections of refugees and a digital economy. The following analysis builds on the three country case studies of Lebanon, Kenya, and Germany to develop wider observations from a comparative perspective. It will first summarize the country-specific insights to then identify major trends and characteristics that define digital livelihoods among refugees and their incorporation into a digital economy more generally at a global level.

Digital Refugee Livelihoods in Lebanon, Kenya, and Germany

Despite having been the starting point for many pioneering programs, Lebanon has become a deathbed for digital livelihoods initiatives and presents one of the most challenging contexts for connecting refugees to digital and remote work. The list of barriers simply seems too long: Syrian refugees have explicitly been excluded from digital livelihood programs and banking, digital financial services are underdeveloped, and the country remains blacklisted by major digital payment providers, while internet connectivity is highly expensive and unreliable. A severe financial and economic crisis has skyrocketed inflation, devalued the national currency, and further undermined the ability of refugee workers to cash out money earned remotely. In the shadows of a failed economy, a vision of digital money and cryptocurrencies that can store value outside of the financial system is finding resonance in a population that has been abandoned by banks and the state.

The effects of multiple intersecting crises not only dramatically increased the need for alternative job opportunities in the affected population but also severely limited how digital jobs could feasibly be used to support those in need. The case of Lebanon underlines that the digital economy is unable to be inclusive of refugees and crisis-affected populations in the most challenging contexts, as it reproduces and intensifies the inequalities that marginalize displaced people and crisis-affected populations at the local level. Restricted by national laws and local practices, excluded from digital skills training and employment opportunities, while suffering under the heavy burden of an economic crisis, refugees in Lebanon exemplify the predicament of displaced people whose lack of local rights and inclusion is mirrored by a condition of digital exile.

Refugees in Kenya also face substantial barriers and challenges as they engage with a digital economy, but unlike Lebanon, mobile money is widely available, and the country's wider digital transformation is considered a success story. The growth of online gig work among refugees in Kenya has been enabled by a range of programs and initiatives that successfully built on the country's well-developed digital ecosystem to tap into a transnational digital economy. Online freelancers working from Kenya's refugee camps have become role models for "entrepreneurial" success under extreme conditions, while also establishing innovative worker collectives through freelancing agencies that mediate between individual workers and clients. For all its successes, the growing digital refugee economy in Kenya also gives cause for concern, as online gig work becomes the digital extension of an informal and insecure labor market that is fraught with risks. Moreover, some refugees' regulatory exclusion from financial services and digital platforms, largely due to problems with identification, pressure them into adopting risky workarounds and informal tactics of economic survival. These include the use of financial and platform accounts with fake IDs and credentials that are not registered in their own name, exposing them to risks of exploitation by intermediaries and the risk of being locked out of accounts and earnings. Scams and cybercrime have become rampant, only adding to the many risks that are associated with gig work.

While digital exclusion and barriers to meaningful connectivity continue to prevent some refugees in Kenya from accessing digital livelihood opportunities, it is their precarious and insecure inclusion into a digital economy that becomes a key driver of risks and vulnerabilities. In a particular form of adverse digital incorporation,[8] their positionality as refugees intersects with the precarity of online freelance work to inscribe new vulnerabilities and risks into the experienced condition of exile. Time-restricted connectivity in camps and the pressures and time zones of a global digital labor market further drive work practices that impact their health and mental health, showing how refugees living in camps are not only spatially bounded but also restricted in terms of time.

Considering the coding schools for refugees and migrants in Berlin against the more challenging backdrop of Lebanon and Kenya can seem like an odd comparison, but it is precisely the combination of differences and similarities that makes their juxtaposition insightful. It is true that refugee coding school participants in Berlin have a realistic prospect of finding decent employment. For them to succeed, however, they often must endure rejections, be resilient amid discrimination, accept un- or underpaid traineeships, and give in to pressures to adapt to the specific culture of the tech sector, all the while being expected to become "good refugees" who work hard and integrate into the German society and economy. In this context, learning how to code symbolizes a way to restore the loss of professional identity and class position that often goes hand in hand with forced displacement, promoting digital careers as an accelerated form of economic integration that can circumvent barriers of the traditional sectors of the labor market.

In this sense, becoming computer programmers and other digitally skilled specialists resembles both an acceleration and a leapfrogging opportunity for refugees, a step up and a thrust forward. Not unlike the promises of online freelancing and digital work in Lebanon and Kenya, these digital career pathways instill strong aspirations in refugees who are willing to accept challenges and make sacrifices on their way toward the desired outcome. These widespread aspirations are fueled by powerful visions and promises of a digital economy that is inclusive and hypermobile and has the potential to liberate refugees from the predicaments of forced displacement.

Visions of Inclusivity, Hypermobility, and Digital Liberation

The promotion of digital skills training and digitally mediated work among refugees is guided by implicit visions of inclusivity, mobility, and liberation. Indeed, refugees and the organizations that support them often come to perceive the informality of the digital economy as a factor that aids access to jobs and economic inclusion despite evident barriers. In the case of online freelance work, such informality includes the seeming ease with which workers can set up profiles and start bidding for jobs posted anywhere in the world, without the need for the bureaucratic processes, work permits, or formal qualifications that often characterize formal employment in the local economy. In countries where refugees have restricted labor market access, remote platform work is seen as both inclusive and invisible, with a capacity to circumvent regulatory restrictions and bureaucratic hurdles. However, as the case of Lebanon underlines, regulations and government intervention into the space of digital refugee livelihoods can result in their exclusion from training and earning opportunities.

This perceived promise of inclusivity goes hand in hand with the idea that the digital economy is hypermobile: a spatial mobility that can transcend nation-state borders and the boundaries of refugee camps virtually, as part of a "shrinking distance imaginary."[9] Some of these ideas are rooted in older metaphors about the mobile and connective qualities of the internet, such as the "information superhighway metaphor" in the 1980s and 90s and its linkage to the "electronic marketplace" metaphor. Such archetypical metaphors and "internet dreams" have long inspired visions about what individuals and societies want to become through their engagement with digital technologies.[10] Visions of digital economic hypermobility are rooted in a conception of mobility as a source of positive change and improvement, even as it also creates and reinforces differences and inequalities.[11] As a transnational digital economy intersects with the concrete lifeworld of refugees in specific settings, some of the most regulated and restricted populations in the world become entangled with one of the least regulated and most interconnected spheres of economic exchange.

Against this backdrop, refugees can perceive the digital economy as a gateway to accelerated social and upward mobility that can offer a shortcut to employment, potentially crossing class boundaries for individuals or leapfrogging across developmental stages in the ways that many African countries envision it in their digital transformation strategies.[12] Refugees and migrants in Berlin saw coding and digital careers as a relatively quick way to reconstitute their professional identity and class status, while refugees in Kenya often envision online freelancing as a potential enabler of the transformation from the "life of a refugee" to that of a successful professional. In crisis-stricken Lebanon, Syrian refugees looked at the digital economy as a possible lifeline and as an escape from the severely restricted economic opportunities they find locally.

As Dragana Kaurin writes in a report on space and imagination in refugee's digital access, "In contrast to the restrictions in mobility and access to physical spaces, the Internet and the digital realm are often framed as a borderless and egalitarian space, and therefore presented as an attractive and viable solution to various challenges refugees face."[13] Refugees are often especially susceptible to these visions of inclusivity and hypermobility because of the exclusion, discrimination, and, in some cases, desperation they encounter. What refugees in a given country or context aspire to depends on their rights and opportunities in this very context: While refugees in Lebanon and Kenya aspired to become online freelance workers due to the absence of formal employment opportunities, Syrians in the city of Berlin were largely immune to the promises of gig work because they had an unrestricted right to work and a realistic expectation to find a formal job in the local tech sector. Digital skills training programs and the wider digital economy can therefore inspire powerful hopes and dreams of different economic lives away from the tribulations and challenges of forced displacement.

The success stories of pioneers like the Somali freelance translators in the Dadaab camp often come to embody these dreams as figures of mobility and digital liberation, who succeed as some of "the most extreme entrepreneurs on the planet."[14] The radiance of their success motivates others to follow in their path. A *figure* can represent an ideal-type persona while also reflecting a particular lived experience.[15] It is "a real person who also is a symbol that embodies the structures of feeling of a particular time and place."[16] While only very few refugees become fully employed and economically self-reliant through digital jobs and online work, an imaginary about the very possibility to succeed inspires hopes among a far larger part of the refugee population, many of whom eventually fail to turn digital learning into digital earning due to the many barriers and challenges discussed throughout this book.

As the perceived inclusivity and hypermobility of a digital economy meets the restrictive context refugees face locally, the digital outsourcing of remote work to refugees who have a limited freedom to move can become a self-fulfilling prophecy that undermines their mobility.[17] These dynamics are similar to an outsourcing model that emerged in the "Third World" at a time when capital mobility created new conditions for the mobility of labor,[18] a process that has been accelerated by digitalization because work now travels transnationally at ease, even though workers often stay put. In a similar vein, digital livelihood initiatives mobilize work rather than refugees, thereby responding to the immobility of people with the hypermobility of digital labor. Rather than becoming the world's next "digital nomads" whose digitally mediated work is underpinned by the freedom of mobility and economic privileges, refugees living in restrictive regimes and spaces could be at risk of gradually forming a globally dispersed mass of precarious workers, whose main reason for accepting the risks and uncertainty of gig work is the absence of equal rights, decent work opportunities, and freedoms.

The Intimacy Between Digital Liberation and Refugees' Ghettoization

Refugees are susceptible to dreams of digital liberation and virtual mobility because they often live with multiple layers of restriction and confinement, be it the physical boundaries of a refugee camp or the boundaries that regulations and policies draw around their limited worlds of opportunity. How a digital sphere that is perceived as hypermobile intersects with these limited worlds tells us something about the wider relationship between refugees' confinement and the digital economy's role in contexts of forced displacement.

Refugee camps have long been critiqued as an instrument of controlling, confining, and governing refugees as a kind of "undesirable" population.[19] This spatial confinement of camps is further complemented by policies and regulations that restrict the rights and freedoms of refugees in host countries, such as the movement restrictions imposed on refugees in Kenya, or the severe restrictions on Syrian refugees' access to formal employment or business registration in Lebanon. Against this backdrop, the visions of hypermobility that refugees come to associate with a digital labor market that can connect workers and clients at a "planetary" scale[20] across borders reveal a disturbing intimacy between confinement and digital liberation. In the ambivalent experience of refugees who aim to enter this digital economy, two versions of space coexist in tension: the "space of flows" in which digital connectivity enables the kind of simultaneity of social and economic practices at a distance, which Manuel Castells first envisioned in 1996, and the "ghettoization" of refugee space, in the sense of a "relative spatial, socio-legal, cultural and political enclosure."[21] In other words, people facing some of the most restrictive socioeconomic and political regimes and spaces are brought into contact with one of the most interconnected and mobile sectors of the global economy.

The intimacy between the digital economy and processes of ghettoization has been brought into sharp relief in the Gaza Strip, where some 2.1 million Palestinians have lived under a near-complete Israeli and Egyptian blockade for two decades. The blockade followed a long period of "de-development" that undermined the ability of the Palestinian economy in Gaza to grow and expand, destroying the economy's capacity to develop and produce.[22] The near-total destruction of Gaza and the mass displacement caused by Israel's ruthless military campaign from 2023 onward was paralleled by the killing of tens of thousands of Palestinian civilians. It also temporality shattered the hopes of the surviving talented Palestinians from Gaza and their international supporters who had worked hard for over a decade to build a digital economy in this most difficult environment.

In autumn 2024, amid the ongoing carnage, I invited the team of Gaza Sky Geeks (GSG) to the University of Edinburgh for a public talk about the current and future role of a digital economy in Palestine. Created and supported by the humanitarian organization Mercy Corps, GSG emerged from entrepreneurship boot camps in 2011 and gradually transformed into Palestine's leading institution that provided more than 4,000 freelancers, founders, and coders per year with technical training and support to earn an income online and remotely. In the face of extreme spatial confinement and economic limitation, GSG leveraged the hypermobility and inclusivity of a global digital economy for the benefit of Gaza's confined skilled workforce. Israeli airstrikes destroyed or severely damaged the buildings that hosted the initiative's tech hubs in Gaza, and GSG was forced to temporally halt its local operations while trying to expand its work in the West Bank in the meantime.

Yet, even during this period of warfare, forcibly displaced people in Gaza showed extreme resilience by continuing to do online freelance work from makeshift coworking spaces that were set up by another initiative called "Hope Hub." Palestinian professionals such as the English teacher Farida, who was interviewed by The Guardian,[23] made around US$200 a month by translating documents and doing other gig work under constant fear of continuing airstrikes. With electricity being scarce, workers took turns charging their laptops, struggled with unstable internet connectivity, and lost up to 30 percent of their earnings to currency exchange fees and another 10 percent to the commission charged by platforms such as Upwork.

As GSG's director Alan El-Kadhi stated in a report, "Digital work remains one of the few viable opportunities for sustainable and inclusive economic growth in Palestine by allowing individuals and companies to access external markets outside of the local restrictions and bring revenue to Palestine."[24] Reflecting on the context of online freelancers in Gaza alongside the aspirations held by similarly entrapped refugees across a variety of countries, such as Kenya and Lebanon, certainly underlines the significance of online and remote work as a lifeline for populations who suffer under the impact of spatial confinement, movement restrictions, and other forms of territorial occupation or oppression. At the same time, such reflection unavoidably leads to a second, less positive observation: that the digital economy is generating economic activity and profits from the desperation and hopelessness of people who live under confinement in the world's largest "ghettos," such as refugee camps and besieged territories. Digital labor platforms charge commission fees and other costs to destitute refugee workers and those who work from makeshift shelters that are at risk of being hit by aerial bombardments. As much as the digital economy can offer a potential lifeline for forcibly displaced people, it capitalizes on their desperation. Its relevance often only increases as a result of their confinement. As people who are stuck in camps, slums, or under territorial occupation do digital work to subsist and survive, the digital economy has indeed become the "preserve of those with nowhere else to go."[25]

Refugees' experience further shows that the digital economy not only benefits from their ghettoization at the local level, but that it also relegates them into yet another "digital ghetto" that is defined by socio-legal and political enclosures that coexist with promises of hypermobility.[26] The digital economy encloses and restricts refugees even as its proponents claim that it can transcend spatial restrictions and local limitations. It is true that the digital economy may often escape the control of regulation,[27] and it may well be characterized by the removal and absence of institutions, which enables some clients to bypass labor market regulations by hiring self-employed workers all over the world. At the same time, digital platforms and the surrounding ecosystem also fill this "void" by creating new regulated marketplaces and digital or financial systems.[28] While digital platforms have contributed to the informalization of labor markets,[29] they have equally introduced new formalities and regulations that can recreate and amplify the encampment and confinement of refugees' local ghettoization in digital space, despite offering a sense of virtual mobility. These dynamics are part of the processes that reshape the condition of exile into one of digital exile.

The Two-Way Formation of Digital Exile

The local barriers and challenges refugees face in their pursuit of digital livelihoods structure the possibilities and limitations of job creation in a global digital economy. The digital economy's capacity to transcend the limitations of the local context is often cited as a key reason for its relevance in the context of forced displacement. Although workers may now be able to do digital work that originates elsewhere, they still remain firmly "tethered to the places in which they live."[30] Despite its hypermobile character, the transnational digital economy remains grounded in the positionality, place, and wider economic and policy settings of refugees in a given host country. This relationship involves a two-way transfer, whereby the entrapment and limitations of exile become imbricated in digital economies, while the insecurities, challenges, and risks of digital jobs and gig work are transferred into the space of refugee livelihoods at the local level. The concept of digital exile encapsulates this dual process, suggesting that the condition of exile is digitalized while the digital economy becomes a new extension of exile's predicament. Importantly, this two-way transfer involves an amplification of barriers and challenges at both ends: The positionality and context of refugees at the local level deepens the precarity and insecurity of digital jobs and gig work, while the digital economy amplifies the inequalities and vulnerabilities that characterize forced displacement.

As refugees often find themselves either excluded from the digital economy or precariously included within it, such digital exile resembles the state of in-betweenness and marginality that has long defined the lives of those who live with protracted displacement. Some 66 percent of refugees live in protracted situations of at least five years in a low- and middle-income host country, and many more face prolonged exile in high-income countries.[31] As long-term displacement foregrounds the need for economic inclusion and rights beyond short-term humanitarian relief, a recurring tension between refugees' economic exclusion and their need for rights and integration often defines the enduring experience of exile and the ongoing forms of confinement and restriction that shape it.[32] This includes the ongoing restrictions and risks that emanate from refugees' incorporation into a digital economy.

Against this backdrop, the meaning of *digital exiles* is twofold: First, it suggests that the lives and livelihoods of refugees are increasingly impacted by digital technology and increasingly shaped by both the opportunities and risks of digital jobs and gig work. As the experience of exile is impacted by digital transformation, some of the characteristics of a digital economy increasingly define the livelihood strategies of refugees. The second part of the meaning behind digital exile refers to the formation of a new space of exile within the digital economy, which involves a kind of digitally mediated marginality produced by overlapping processes of categorical exclusion and precarious inclusion. Such exclusion is categorical because many of the barriers that refugees face, as they seek to access digital jobs or services, are linked to their unique positionality and status as forcibly displaced people and their identity as refugees with certain nationalities. At the same time, their inclusion into the digital economy, if it succeeds at all, is precarious and fraught with insecurities and risks. Such "adverse digital incorporation" emphasizes how the inclusion of marginalized populations into digital systems can create new inequalities and risks, while also deepening preexisting inequalities and vulnerabilities.[33]

This digital exile of refugees by means of regulations, exclusive practices, and policies also has spatial and temporal dimensions. In spatial terms, refugees can be marginalized in the transnational digital economy due to the limitations they encounter as displaced people living in specific locations, host countries, and refugee camps. Their entrapment in a refugee camp makes refugees especially susceptible to the imaginary of a hypermobile transnational digital economy, and it simultaneously limits their capacity to benefit from it. In terms of time, we have seen how the temporality of time-restricted electricity and internet provision in Kenya's camps can prevent refugees from accessing job postings uploaded in the time zones of the dominant buyer markets such as the United States. In a similar vein, Syrian refugees in Lebanon's Shatila camp are "forced to adapt their sleeping patterns to the needs of firms on the other side of the planet and in different time zones," spending their nights labeling data used to develop AI.[34] Moreover, digital skills training and careers suggest a possible acceleration of time and social mobility, as an ostensible shortcut to employment that often ends up not being so short after all because it is fraught with barriers and obstacles. Some Syrian participants of coding schools in Berlin experienced this tension between the speed of digital transformation and the challenges that keep on thrusting them backward.

All of this illustrates newly emerging temporal dynamics of exile under the impact of digitalization. Long described as a rupture in time as much as in space,[35] exile can involve a suspended existence in the meanwhile. This frequently involves experiences of prolonged waiting, uncertainty about one's status, the foreclosure of any security about one's future, and the limbo between a lost country in a lost past and the need to move on and become someone new. Refugees' experience in a digital economy reveals new rifts between the hypermobility, speed, and temporal synchroneity of a planetary digital market on the one hand, and the restricted, disrupted, and suspended temporality in which refugees often find themselves in on the other.

An ostensibly inclusive and hypermobile digital economy rarely transcends the restrictive local condition and positionality of refugees. More commonly, it absorbs their positionality in unproductive ways and excludes them based on their identity and status. Despite its association with informality and a lack of regulations, the digital economy imposes a set of formal identity-related barriers on refugees: Regulations exclude those with unrecognized IDs from SIM-card registrations, financial services, and platforms, while international sanctions can lead to the systematic financial and digital exclusion of entire nationalities, such as Syrians. Even once included and successfully active on digital labor platforms, many refugees who lack the means to prove their identity face ongoing problems and risks. In Kenya, refugee online freelancers often use proxy identities and buy platform accounts registered by someone else while hiding their own true identities. Faced with insurmountable barriers to establish a digital presence as who they really are, these individuals therefore cease to exist as a recognized "real" person. They experience the dilemma of either being excluded from the platform economy or becoming incorporated as invisible, rightless, and exploitable workers. The digital economy can thereby mirror and further deepen the lack of recognition and rights refugees have encountered in host countries for many years.

Embracing Risks and Shifting Mindsets

The digital economy and digital livelihood programs in the aid sector have diversified the risks that affect refugees while also expecting them to take risks and make insecure investments on their pathway to self-reliance. This pattern extends a long-standing process of framing them as entrepreneurial subjects and independent economic agents who are "'self-helped' individuals with an entrepreneurial and hardworking spirit."[36] As I will discuss in more detail below, this process has involved strategic attempts to transform their "mentality" and "mindsets" toward one that is more aligned with digital careers and gig work.

Digital skills and livelihoods programs often demand a range of material and immaterial investments from refugees, which can entail new risks and insecurities. As digital livelihoods and digital training programs instill a hopeful vision of change and success in refugee participants, they invest time and resources, purchase devices and pay for pricey data plans, or take leave from work and family; refugee graduates of Berlin's coding schools often start out in unpaid or underpaid internships, while online freelance workers in Kenya invest countless hours of unpaid labor time to build a reputation in platforms and apply for gigs. They also invest into secondhand platform accounts registered on someone else's name, only to find themselves locked out of their earnings due to recurring suspicions of fraud. Digital refugee workers in Lebanon reported selling goods and borrowing money to survive during the country's economic crisis, some saying they sold household goods and borrowed money to buy computers and make other investments into their digital livelihood journeys. These and other investments entail significant financial risk if the aspired returns from training programs and digital jobs do not materialize. A digital risk epidemic among refugees is further spread by the precarious and insecure character of the digital economic activities that aid organizations and enterprises promote, often without sufficient focus on protecting beneficiaries from the resulting harm.[37] Among refugee online freelancers, this includes a range of scams and cybercrimes, and exploitation by brokers and intermediaries, as well as the negative impact from insecure and high-pressure gig work on their health and mental health.

In the face of all these risks, it is no surprise that many refugees do not consider digital jobs and online work to be a safe option for them. Others are unwilling or unable to make the continuous investments and take the risks of an entrepreneurial journey without any security of returns. Digital jobs can also be seen as less prestigious or accepted by family members and the wider community that surrounds refugees, compared to more traditional jobs and employment. These and other factors are often cited when aid organizations and enterprises supporting refugees talk of a need to change refugees' mindsets, which takes on a particular dynamic in the field of digital refugee livelihoods.

Along the pathway from learning to earning, digital skills training and digital jobs involve an attempted remaking of "refugees" and their "mindsets," so they embrace the specific ideological, cultural, and entrepreneurial underpinnings of these trajectories.

They should become less risk-averse, more hardworking, and highly motivated. The stories of refugees who embrace the need for self-sufficiency in gig work and coding while trying to change their "mindsets" are embedded in a wider transformation in humanitarian aid and development: a shift away "from emphasizing the placement of refugees into formal work . . . to promoting refugees' informal work through livelihoods training and entrepreneurship today."[38] Digitalization has accelerated this shift toward a kind of gig entrepreneurship, which carries the risks of entrepreneurship but entails little of its freedom and glamour.

Organizations running digital livelihood programs for refugees often contrasted the required entrepreneurial mindset with a "refugee mentality" that some aid workers have associated with idleness or lethargy due to aid reliance. Because such mentality is "seen as detrimental to building self-reliant, resilient and responsible subjects," self-reliance can only liberate refugees from dependency if they also shift their mindset.[39] As a program manager of a prominent digital livelihoods initiative in Kenya told me in a meeting, "Beyond skills, shaping the mindset is the greatest difficulty. Our support mechanisms are oriented around how to shift the mindset for freelancers. They have access to short-term unsustainable opportunities in the camps, that bring in some money—then you need to make them aware of this shift, that they need to invest some time, maybe have no income for a month, but then making money from that freelancing for a long time. To shape that mindset is often the hardest part."

As digital livelihood initiatives cannot change the terms and conditions of platform work, the digital economy reshapes the conditions of livelihoods provision more than aid organizations can reshape its disempowering effects.[40] Part of this process is the social conditioning of refugees to act and think in a way that matches the terms and business models of digital labor platforms, as well as accepting the underlying risks. Refugees who were described by aid organizations as having unrealistic expectations about pay needed to recalibrate those expectations. As the program manager further explained, "When we get jobs for them, they think we have the power to negotiate how much they are paid. It's not the case but they think that. But then, when we are paying them less, they think we can negotiate it. They think if I do one job very good, I need to be paid the same for the next job, but freelancing does not work like that. It's a lot of communication involved to make them realize all that." As many similar programs around the world try to tap into the earning potential of a digital economy, they see a need to adequately prepare refugees for the demands of an online gig economy. As part of this process, they do not only teach them technical skills but also try to reorient their mindset toward one that positively values the significant investments of training and unpaid labor time, while also accepting low levels of pay, as part of their journey.

In a similar vein, refugee coders in Berlin were expected to be hardworking and highly motivated. As powerful appeals to their passion and entrepreneurialism are mobilized toward a desired future goal, all investments and sacrifices are expected to pay off and increase one's status eventually, as a kind of "aspirational labour."[41] Industry experts described refugees as especially "hungry" for tech jobs, which made them more hardworking than stereotypically "lazy" and "comfortable" locals. Refugees were framed as perfect for the kind of transformation a digital economy demanded, even though their perceived cultural differences often became an obstacle due to discrimination and pressures to conform with the working culture of the digital economy. The often-cited need for strong "soft skills" indirectly suggests a need for sociocultural adaptation to become a better "culture fit" for a self-consciously cosmopolitan tech scene that has its own sociocultural norms.

Desperation and the Search of Respect

Why did the mostly middle-class refugees who participated in coding schools in Berlin not aspire to become online gig workers? Because they could realistically find decent local employment. Why do refugees in Kenya's camps and in Lebanon's crisis-affected economy, including the highly educated, aspire to become self-employed gig workers? Because they have very few local alternatives and rarely because it is their professional dream. The aspiration to become an online "freelancer" is not so "free" after all. It is rooted in the local inequalities that affect refugees and the global inequalities that undermine development in low- and middle-income countries, where most platform workers are based.

Desperation not only makes refugees susceptible to the digital economy's promises but also makes them more vulnerable to scams and cybercrime. This became clear in the workshop we organized in Nairobi, with one of the refugee participants saying that "desperation makes you click on those links" and another one adding that scammers "know refugees are desperate." In an ideal scenario where refugees have the unconditional right to formal employment in a healthy local economy, with freedom of movement and access to educational opportunities, online gig work is unlikely to inspire the hopes and dreams it currently does in restrictive contexts of forced displacement. For Syrian refugees in the highly limiting context of crisis-stricken Lebanon, digital skills training and digital work came to embody aspirations and hopes precisely because of the tribulations and hopelessness they faced locally. The choices behind refugees' digital livelihood journeys are therefore highly constrained and form a mutually constitutive relationship with their marginalization and exclusion from dignified employment in the respective host countries.

Even in the context of mostly well-educated coding school students in Berlin, the initial motivation to sign up for courses and pursue a new career path was often rooted in the challenges they faced in local employment, including the bureaucratic barriers that prevented them from working in their previous professions. Moreover, the wider experience of being disrespected and discriminated strengthened the appeal of digital jobs as a possible shortcut to economic integration and professional success. As one student at the ReDI coding school in Berlin said, when asked about the students' motivation to take the course, it is about getting respect, "because no one respects us. We feel like cockroaches here."

Epilogue

Working Toward an Inclusive and Fair Future of Digital Refugee Work

Critical research can be an important catalyst for change, raising suspicion about established assumptions and highlighting where things do not work as well as they should. It is equally important to think about how the implications of critical research can inform positive change in the future. This epilogue is intended to do just that, aiming to discuss the wider implications of the research in this book for current and future practice while offering ideas and frameworks that can help guide different actors in the process.

Despite the many challenges I discussed in this book, digital livelihoods initiatives have been versatile in adapting to the circumstances of different local contexts, often by innovating solutions for locally specific problems and helping refugees to overcome barriers along their digital economy journeys. Examples for such innovations are refugee freelancing agencies and social impact platforms and enterprises that build bridges across the divide between individual refugees and a competitive digital economy. Programs and initiatives have responded to a widening digital skills gap with training programs, innovated feasible payment solutions to counter financial exclusion, and convinced corporations and employers to provide paid work to refugees, all the while offering a wide range of additional support such as digital equipment, mentoring, career coaching, and on-the-job training. Building on this wealth of initiatives, some advocacy efforts have also convinced policymakers to revise regulations so that refugees have better access to digital tools and services, including mobile money.[1] All of these efforts combined have kept the digital economy alive and running for refugees and thereby upheld the powerful aspirations it continues to instill in them.

That the digital economy now encompasses some of the world's most economically and politically marginalized populations, such as forcibly displaced people, raises complicated questions for initiatives and organizations that support them and aim to protect them from harm. The widespread adoption of digital tools in humanitarian aid makes "do no digital harm" an important imperative.[2] Connecting refugees to insecure forms of digital labor that expose them to new risks raises urgent questions about the involved actors' capacity to meet this imperative in practice. More attention should therefore be paid to both inclusion and protection: how refugees can be supported to access work in the digital economy and how they can be protected once they participate in it.

An inclusive digital economy for refugees requires accessible infrastructures and connectivity, with a need for people to be financially included and have recognized identification documents. It further requires improved connectivity in refugee camps and affordable devices, alongside the development of digital skills.[3] Importantly, inclusiveness demands extra efforts to empower specific groups that are discriminated against and excluded in the digital labor market.[4] Key areas of a functioning digital economy, such as policies and regulations, infrastructures, innovation, and skills, therefore require a coherent focus on inclusion of underserved segments of the population, such as women and refugees.[5]

Inclusion must be accompanied by improved rights and protections for workers, which will contribute to fairer conditions in the digital economy. At the level of labor standards, a fair digital economy requires mechanisms, regulations, and institutions that protect workers and preserve their rights while addressing current decent work deficits and precarious working conditions. There is a further need to ensure that communities can exercise their human rights online; they should also be protected from risks in a digital economy.[6] This includes the risks that can result from connectivity and digital economic activity, which requires legal and regulatory frameworks, safeguards, and protection from cybercrimes and other risks. There is a specific need to protect refugees through facilitating safe and secure digitally enabled livelihoods and opportunities for decent work free of exploitation.[7]

The ILO's Centenary Declaration on the Future of Work highlighted the importance of "harnessing the fullest potential of technological progress and productivity growth, including through social dialogue, to achieve decent work and sustainable development, which ensure dignity, self-fulfillment and a just sharing of the benefits for all."[8] Under the framework of a human-centered agenda, technological change should be aligned with decent work and social justice.[9] Accordingly, all workers should enjoy adequate protection in accordance with the "Decent Work Agenda," taking into account respect for their fundamental rights, an adequate minimum wage, maximum limits on working time, and safety and health at work.[10] The realities of refugees who work in digital and remote jobs, especially those in low- and middle-income countries with large informal economies, seem somewhat distant from the principles set out in this vision.

Some of the specific vulnerabilities and needs of refugees in a digital economy are addressed by UNHCR's Digital Transformation Strategy, which identifies priority outcomes for a digital future of displaced communities. The strategy emphasizes inclusion through "equitable access to digital technology," "opportunities for lifelong learning," and "inclusion in the digital economy"; it also demands protection from "digital risk," enabling refugees to have "access to trusted channels, avoid harm and have agency in decision-making." It further identifies a need for "access to high quality, efficient and safe digital services."[11] Expanding fair practices in the digital economy must go hand in hand with wider improvements in the legal and regulatory framework that can allow refugees to fully participate in economic activities.[12] Areas of emerging good practices for decent and inclusive platform work include facilitating access to work, providing opportunities to build skills and expertise, improving working conditions, and reducing work-related risks or costs.[13] Initiatives that seek to promote fair and safe digital livelihoods among refugees should aim at generating a kind of "self-reliance" that is "grounded in basic protections and human rights, including the right to decent work, because it otherwise risks being defined by economic insecurity, exploitation and marginalization."[14]

The Five Pillars of an Inclusive and Fair Digital Economy for Refugees

Building on the two principles of inclusion and protection, an inclusive and fair digital economy for refugees rests on at least five pillars: (1) inclusive and meaningful connectivity, (2) financial inclusion and digital identity, (3) skills and capabilities, (4) fair working conditions and rights, and (5) cyber safety and digital risk mitigation. I originally developed a similar version of these five pillars over the course of research I did with the ILO and UNHCR, in part by leading a two-year research and consultancy project into the opportunities and challenges of the digital economy for refugees across eight countries (Kenya, Uganda, Ethiopia, Sudan, Egypt, Jordan, Lebanon, Iraq). While the following discussion of the pillars will focus on the country studies covered in this book, their relevance is rooted in wider comparative evidence from a global cross-country perspective.

Pillar 1: Inclusive and Meaningful Connectivity

While universal connectivity for all covers the basic provision of internet access, the notion of meaningful connectivity refers to a safe, productive, and affordable online experience.[15] Access to such meaningful connectivity is a foundational precondition for refugees to participate in the digital economy and benefit from its income-generating opportunities. It can also increase their capacity to use online training and skills development opportunities. Unfortunately, refugees face wide-ranging connectivity challenges, including a lack of broadband affordability, smartphones, and computers relative to income, as well as unreliable and disrupted connectivity. Regulations that require identification documents for registering SIM cards pose another barrier for many refugees, often triggering the need for informal workarounds that can entail risks.

These challenges are very evident in both Lebanon and Kenya, where refugees face identity-related barriers to registering SIM cards while also struggling with the high costs of internet connectivity and digital devices. Unreliable and disrupted electricity posed another challenge for aspiring digital refugee workers in both countries, albeit in different ways: While Lebanon's internet provision was heavily impacted by the economic crisis and the associated collapse of digital infrastructures, refugees in Kenya's camps were dependent on community centers or costly mobile data for connectivity while also struggling with time-restricted availability of the internet. Moreover, digital skills training graduates and digital workers often did not own their own computers and were either unable to access a device or had to borrow one from family members or friends. While a limited range of online learning and digital work opportunities can function through mobile connectivity and smartphones, these were no less costly to operate.

Pillar 2: Financial Inclusion and Digital Identity

Access to financial services and digital payment channels is a foundational requirement for refugees to make a digital livelihood, which also requires them to have widely recognized forms of identification. However, regulations that require a certain kind of ID and other documentation can prevent refugees from opening accounts with banks and other financial service providers. This largely concerns KYC regulations and their connection to Anti-Money Laundering and Combating the Financing of Terrorism policies, which require financial service providers to identify customers and ensure they do not violate the policies. A lack of recognized digital identity therefore remains a major source of exclusion for refugees in a digital world. While mobile money and fintech solutions are often described as more inclusive than traditional banking, they are not available everywhere, and a range of barriers persist. This includes the need for official IDs when registering accounts with mobile money services and digital wallets. Even if refugees manage to open digital wallets, they often cannot cash out digitally stored money locally, especially where mobile money infrastructures are not widely developed and where regulations require users of digital wallets to have a linked bank account.

Only very few refugees in Kenya held bank accounts, and although mobile money is omnipresent in the country, ID-related barriers for some refugees meant that they depend on brokers or friends to process payments and transfers from online work. In Lebanon, a combination of restrictive national policies, international regulations, and risk-averse banking practices means that only very few can open bank accounts. International sanctions also mean that important US-based and international digital payment services such as PayPal are banned in the country, while also excluding Syrian nationals from opening accounts with financial services and digital platforms. Even Syrian refugees in Europe, including in Germany, faced significant obstacles to opening bank accounts because their identity documents are not recognized and due to risk-averse policies aligned with sanctions and KYC regulations.[16] Although the financial regulator in Germany mandated banks to open accounts for refugees and asylum seekers, they are perceived as a "high-risk" segment by financial service providers.[17]

Humanitarian and development organizations often try to innovate workable alternatives to get aid payments to beneficiaries and allow them to make digital transactions. However, in Kenya as well as in Jordan, this resulted in separate, often limited-purpose financial services that provide "second-rate financial access (i.e., the ability to use specific financial instruments) without inclusion (i.e., incorporation into existing, mainstream financial systems on the same terms as host populations)," resulting in a form of "financial encampment" that deepens inequalities rather than transforming them.[18]

Pillar 3: Skills and Capabilities

Access to digital skills and other skills that are needed to flourish in a digital economy is a key enabler for people to benefit from digitalization, but there is a wide gap between the skills most refugees hold and those demanded by the digital economy. Forcibly displaced people often face disrupted educational trajectories, can be excluded from training opportunities in host countries, and often require rapid reskilling if their preexisting qualifications are not recognized. Although digital skills training initiatives supporting refugees have emerged in most major refugee-hosting countries, the journey from learning to earning is often fraught with obstacles and uncertainties, requiring refugees to take financial risks, invest unpaid labor time, and shift their "mindset" to fit the demands of digital jobs or gig work.

The research on Kenya and Lebanon covered in this book made clear that graduates of training programs often felt inadequately equipped to compete for jobs in a digital economy and on digital labor platforms, suggesting a lack of ongoing support mechanisms and a need for continuous and more in-depth programs that go beyond teaching basic or intermediate skills. In a similar vein, among coding school students in Berlin, the perception was often that even after several cycles of training, their capabilities did not match the skill profiles demanded by jobs in the tech sector. Equipping refugees with the skills needed to flourish in a digital world of work requires both technical digital skills and other skills for a digital economy, including English language skills and so-called soft skills. Importantly, digital literacy and digital skills are not only a prerequisite of digital inclusion but also essential for protection and safeguarding against digital risks and online harm.[19] This became particularly evident among refugees in Kenya, who reported being exposed to a wide range of scams and digital risks. Their experience underlines the need to incorporate digital safety modules into all digital skills programs.[20]

Pillar 4: Fair Working Conditions and Rights

In some refugee-hosting countries with an enabling policy environment and a strong economy, such as Germany, digital jobs can offer an important alternative employment pathway for refugees who face challenges in finding local employment. Moreover, online freelance work can provide refugees in many host countries with access to a digital labor market that is somewhat independent from locally experienced employment restrictions. Despite these opportunities, the working conditions in the platform economy are widely inadequate to support potentially vulnerable and marginalized populations such as refugees. Some of the risks associated with digital labor platforms include "debt traps" if platform workers' costs exceed their earnings,[21] task-specific risks of injury and accidents for location-based workers, exposure to harmful materials, mental illness, and loneliness among online freelance workers.[22] Refugee freelance workers often face low pay with insecure and irregular income while having to invest unpaid labor time and financial resources; they lack the benefits of employment and commonly do not have access to insurance, social protection, and other benefits; they are exposed to exploitation and risks, including the risk of non-payment by clients; and they experience negative impacts to their health and mental health, all the while being isolated and unsupported by unions or other collective worker organizations.

Improving working conditions for refugees in the digital economy will require attention to areas such as minimum pay, contracts and policies on working conditions, insurance, dispute mediation, and collective bargaining.[23] While campaigning in Europe has reached important achievements for the rights of some platform workers, such as the EU Directive on Platform Work,[24] the digital economy remains largely unregulated in low- and middle-income countries, and especially so with regards to refugees. While the absence of rights and protection mechanisms for refugees in the digital economy hints at a need for regulations and formalization, steps toward formalization—such as tax registration or identification requirements—often lead to new barriers and risks, as the case of refugees in Kenya underlined. Due to the specific needs and vulnerabilities of forcibly displaced populations, the struggle for fairer working conditions in the digital economy must be combined with assurances that any new regulations, policies, and laws do not exclude refugees and asylum seekers who may not be able to meet the underlying requirements. Protection and inclusion need to go hand in hand.

Pillar 5: Cyber Safety and Digital Risk Mitigation

Digital risks affecting refugees include social media hacking, mobile money fraud, cyber bullying, government surveillance, and a wide range of scams, including those pretending to facilitate resettlement.[25] Cybercriminals often take advantage of poorly secured, outdated, or unlicensed technology in many developing countries and among refugee populations, which can be compounded by a lack of digital skills and effective cybersecurity education.[26] Those who find themselves in a dire economic situation are particularly susceptible to the false promises of scams, which exploit their desperation. A specific source of digitally mediated risk for refugees results from their regulatory exclusion from digital and financial services, including through identification requirements. Such exclusion pressures some to innovate alternatives and informal workarounds, as in Kenya for example, where refugee online workers pay for access to "secondhand" SIM cards, financial accounts, and digital platform accounts that are registered with someone else's identity and details. In addition to costly fees and a risk of exploitation by intermediaries, these practices expose them to the risk of account deactivation and resulting financial losses. Refugees who fall victim to scams, cybercrime, and exploitation in the digital economy are unlikely to report these for fear of repercussions on their status, making them especially vulnerable to their effects.

Increasing online safety and digital risk mitigation capacities among refugees who participate in the digital economy requires specific training and skills development, such as digital safeguarding modules to accompany any digital livelihoods program. However, their participation in a digital economy will not be safe unless it is enshrined in inclusive policies, rights, and protections that address the underlying barriers and challenges that expose them to online harm and digital risks in the first place.

Emerging Models and Innovative Approaches

The promotion of digital jobs and remote work among refugees has involved collaborations across conventional boundaries between a large variety of actors, including humanitarian and development organizations, social enterprises, digital platforms, technology companies and mobile network operators, training providers, universities, and governments, among others. The complexity of how digital economies intersect with different policy areas and fields of practice across local, national, and international scales often means that a single actor can only operate within clearly defined limits. For example, effective digital skills training requires post-training support and links to employers and digital platforms that can ensure job placement. Accessing such work, however, might require technology companies to provide computers and development organizations to set up internet-equipped workspaces among refugees and in camps. Digital labor platforms may need to be convinced that recognizing nonstandard identification documents held by refugees is a risk worth taking. Scaling up remote work for refugees in a certain country or region might require policy changes, such as easing ID requirements for refugees' access to financial services so they can get paid digitally. Programs and initiatives also need to be evidence-based, and innovation must be grounded in the realities people experience on the ground, all of which requires research by universities and other research organizations.

While the struggle for inclusion, improved rights, and better working conditions among refugees in a digital economy is a long-term process, several important models have emerged to build bridges and work across barriers and challenges in the meantime. Often connected to digital skills training, these models include social impact platforms and enterprises (SIPEs), as well as freelancing collectives and agencies. Their intermediation between refugees and a digital economy helps connect individual workers to paid work while incubating them in a safe and supportive environment and cushioning them from some forms of exploitation and risks in the online gig economy.[27] Some initiatives have started to organize digital refugee workers collectively as part of wider online worker associations. Alongside a large diversity of specific interventions and actions by other stakeholders, these emerging models and actors contributed to some improvements across the five pillars of an inclusive and fair digital economy for refugees.

Social Impact Platforms and Enterprises

SIPEs have provided an important alternative for training and job creation by acting as bridge-builders and intermediaries between refugees and a wider digital economy. Usually operating at a relatively small scale, SIPEs can partner with training providers in refugee-hosting countries while acquiring paid work and projects from business partners and clients, which are then distributed to cohorts of trained workers who are also being offered other forms of assistance and support. While some of these platforms and enterprises acquire outsourced sets of digital labor tasks from business clients, others use digital tools to mediate between clients and workers who do forms of work that are not necessarily digital in nature. As businesses with a social impact mission, SIPEs are strategically situated between the private sector and the aid sector.

Prominent examples of social impact platforms and enterprises that support refugees in making a digital livelihood are Humans in the Loop, Na'amal, NaTakallam, and Equal Reach. Their business models offer an alternative to directly exposing refugees to fierce competition on major freelancing platforms. They do so by forming their own incubated environment within which trainees and workers are supported and mentored while also ensuring they are paid adequately and are not exploited. For example, the language service provider NaTakallam has avoided existing corporate platforms by matching clients with workers directly, thereby allowing them to control the pricing of services and other aspects of the relationship. Moreover, enterprises like the Bulgaria-based Humans in the Loop have committed themselves to a Fair Work Policy that aims to provide an ethical and safe working environment for their beneficiaries. The policy covers aspects such as minimum pay, clear communication with workers, equitable recruitment, and equitable distribution of jobs among workers and partners.[28] Partnerships with local NGOs and training providers allow enterprises like Humans in the Loop to train and recruit workers across different countries. Such partnerships also help overcome challenges such as a lack of digital financial services, using local partners to distribute money local workers earned through Humans in the Loop.

Whether or not these models are scalable to encompass a larger mass of refugee workers remains to be seen, since the vetted and trained workers at smaller initiatives also require a lot of investment and "hyper-local support," as Giselle Gonzales, the CEO of Equal Reach, phrased it in an online conference. Examples for such support would be working out alternative payment solutions for refugee workers without financial service accounts, providing training and mentoring, or supporting them to access digital devices and internet connectivity. Some of these services and support mechanisms could be digitalized or automated to allow initiatives to scale up. Combining such "hyper-local" support with operations at a larger international scale is challenging and would likely require substantial resources as well as sustainable and reliable income streams.

The Agency Model

Agencies have become a prominent model for mediating between the constraints of the local context and the digital platform economy. Such an agency can be registered with one or multiple digital labor platforms and can be structured as a private business, an NGO, a cooperative, a collective, or a social enterprise. Agencies can play an important mediating role between refugee workers and platforms by taking on larger projects that can then be distributed to individual workers by purposefully selecting beneficiaries from marginalized backgrounds and by supporting workers to process payments,[29] as well as by establishing relationships with clients and partners as an umbrella organization.

One of the pioneering agencies is the Dadaab Collective Freelancing Agency that came out of the Refugee Employment and Skills Initiative in Kenya. To support graduates of training programs, the agency has acquired projects from clients and distributed them to qualified refugee workers in the camp, who then delivered the work while the agency took a commission of 10 percent from their earnings to enable its continuing support, including training, networking, and mentorship. Although such agencies work through established digital labor platforms, where they can sometimes bid for jobs as a collective, they insert an additional supportive and protective layer into the relationship between individual refugees and a highly competitive and challenging platform economy. Agencies also work as part of an interconnected pathway that includes refugees who take part in training programs in a cohort of alumni who can then become part of the talent pool for which the agency acquires work.[30]

Lorraine Charles, the founder of Na'amal, which trained refugees with partnering organizations in Kenya and Uganda and aimed to connect them to remote jobs, explained how a partnership with the impact sourcing platform Equal Reach led them to adopt the agency model in providing refugees with digital and remote work. "By building the agency, we are able to control and scaffold the talent," said Charles during a session of the 2024 Migration Summit, an online conference.[31] She added, "The idea of the agency is, it de-risks companies. Companies have lots of outsourced projects. . . . So, we thought, how can we take advantage of this to support our talent finding work and meaningful work?" Na'amal officially launched their agency in January 2024 and built it "as a way to prove a model" and bring dignified work to refugees they are training: "We know how good the talent are, we know that they are amazing. But this is something employers don't know. So, by building the agency we are finding a way to showcase the talent while providing them the scaffolding and training they need after finishing the programs. And giving them experience, building their portfolio, so eventually they can go off on their own."[32]

Agencies insert a mediating layer between refugees and the digital economy, a kind of incubated environment with support and mentoring that can cushion vulnerable refugee workers against the risks of a global gig economy marketplace. As Abdi Ambari, the technology lead at Na'amal, said during the session at the Migration Summit, "Once we identified the talent for the work, and match them correctly with the work that needs to be done, then we sit down and map the entire project, together with the talent. . . . Our approach is to always ensure that the talent have all they need to execute the project." As refugee "talents" are often directly thrown into a new project, they need the agency to fill gaps and ensure their work meets the quality to attract further investments from a client. The support can also include innovative solutions to connectivity challenges, which have been an issue in Kenya, said Ambari. In the face of tight deadlines, problems with internet connectivity in refugee camps could mean project failure for an individual refugee worker without support. Na'amal and their partners usually find an "innovative way to get past it," and once refugees earn some money, they are encouraged to invest in better connectivity and devices.[33]

An agency can be effective in pooling refugee workers and trying to attract projects for them, but according to Giselle Gonzales, the founder and CEO of Equal Reach, "the missing piece" between refugee workers and jobs is often a link to companies that offer paying work and search for the skills that refugees have. Equal Reach is trying to fill that gap by "funnelling work opportunities" to refugee workers around the world. "There is this entire hidden industry within most enterprises, all the way down to small business companies where freelancing and contract-based work is an essential part of how they operate," said Gonzales, adding that 54 percent of Google's workforce are freelancers. Their aim is to scale the model but simultaneously offer the kind of hyperlocal support that Na'amal and local partner organizations can bring.[34]

The benefits and downsides of these agencies were also discussed in my meetings with the team of Humans in the Loop. The enterprise received funding from Upwork, which partnered with the Tent Partnership for Refugees, a network of over 250 companies committed to including refugees. Setting up an agency on Upwork was one of the key steps they encouraged. "As an agency, we can also mediate some of the negative effects on the platform, including what work is accepted," said Hester Gartrell, chief impact officer at Humans in the Loop. She also hoped that an agency can help with the payment problems refugee freelancers faced, since an agency could process payments on their behalf and then distribute the income to individual refugees through alternative channels. The partnership with Tent also meant that they had access to a network of companies that already committed to employing refugees.

However, she worried that the business model of digital labor platforms ultimately meant that different refugee agencies ended up competing with each other for a limited pool of available projects, funding, and work. "I have concerns that each of us are doing it from scratch and become competing agencies," said Gartrell. Moreover, a first pilot training as part of the agency, with Ukrainians based in Bulgaria, was described as "challenging," not least because the field of annotation work is highly saturated on Upwork and competition can be fierce.

At a more general level, from the perspective of international labor standards, one could also critique the tendency of these agencies to take commission from workers' earnings to fund their ongoing operations. This is justified since initiatives provide support and services to refugees and other workers, but strictly speaking, it could be interpreted as a violation of ILO Convention No. 181 and its Article 7, which states that agencies should not charge fees and costs to workers for their services.[35]

Campaigning and Worker Organizing

International organizations and researchers continue to demand better working conditions in the gig economy. This ranges from the establishment of new digital labor standards that recognize the unique needs of refugees to the advocacy and action-research of organizations such as the Fair Work Foundation, which holds digital labor platforms accountable and measures their performance against a set of fair work principles. For online work platforms, the five principles are fair pay, fair conditions, fair contracts, fair management, and fair representation. This latter principle has been especially difficult to realize for many platform workers. Only two out of fifteen major web-based digital labor platforms rated by the Fairwork Foundation acknowledged workers' right to freedom of association, but in practice, none of the platforms recognized collective worker bodies or bargained with them.[36] This lack of access to unions and collective bargaining among platform workers contributes to precarity at work, including issues such as unfair compensation, insurance, health and safety hazards, discrimination, and other occupational risks associated with the sector.[37]

As refugee workers are often specifically marginalized, they lack access to traditional means of worker representation. Due to the legal ambivalence that surrounds their status and their participation in a digital economy, refugees may also be reluctant to increase the visibility of their digital and remote work through forms of worker organizing or collective action. National initiatives that organize and support online and platform workers have emerged across a variety of countries, but only few actively reach out to refugees. In Kenya, iWorkers supports and organizes online freelance workers while including marginalized communities such as refugees, with the goal to "harness the collective power of digital workers and build a community bound by shared expertise, experiences and passion."[38] The organization offers free membership for freelancers with benefits, such as access to online courses and workshops, including on mental health and resources for stress management and well-being. They also collaborated with digital skills training initiatives that serve refugees, such as Learning Lions in Kenya's Turkana region, by delivering freelance training workshops. Frida Mwangi, the cofounder of iWorkers, has been a driving force behind creating inclusive digital work opportunities for marginalized populations in Kenya, including for rural women and refugees. Despite the creation of a new union, the Kenya Union of Gig Workers in 2024, she highlighted the challenges of worker organizing in this sector.

"You don't have a clear value proposition or long-term vision that can be translated to a point where members are paying; it is difficult. If you don't have money coming in from members, there is no way to have enough operational funds," she told me in a meeting in March 2025, adding that although iWorkers also offered a premium membership for a fee, none of the almost six hundred members listed on their website are paying. The specific challenges for organizing digital refugee workers include fears about too much visibility, as well as permit requirements that prevented many from officially operating a business. Other factors that undermined worker organizing among refugees in the digital economy have included a lack of awareness that they do have the right to join unions in selected countries and a widespread perception, and experienced reality, that unions do not represent refugees.[39] Going forward, Mwangi highlighted a need to raise more awareness, to provide workers with information about their rights, and to create a vision in which they see the benefits of organizing without fear of negative repercussions.

Notes

Introduction

1. UNHCR, *Kenya: Registered Refugees and Asylum Seekers, as of 31 January 2025* (2025), https://www.unhcr.org/ke/wp-content/uploads/sites/2/2025/02/Kenya-Statistics-Package-31-January-2025.pdf.

2. UNHCR, "Lebanon," accessed March 6, 2025, https://www.unhcr.org/countries/lebanon.

3. UNHCR, "UNHCR Refugee Data Finder," accessed March 18, 2025, https://www.unhcr.org/refugee-statistics.

4. OECD, *A Roadmap Toward a Common Framework for Measuring the Digital Economy. Report for the G20 Digital Economy Task Force* (2020), https://www.itu.int/en/ITU-D/Statistics/Documents/publications/OECDRoadmapDigitalEconomy2020.pdf.

5. Andreas Hackl, ed., *Digital Refugee Livelihoods and Decent Work: Towards Inclusion in a Fairer Digital Economy* (Geneva: International Labour Organization, 2021), https://www.ilo.org/publications/digital-refugee-livelihoods-and-decent-work-towards-inclusion-fairer.

6. UNHCR, "UNHCR Refugee Data Finder," accessed March 2, 2025, https://www.unhcr.org/refugee-statistics.

7. ILO, *Realizing Decent Work in the Platform Economy: International Labour Conference 113th Session, 2025* (2024), 15, https://www.ilo.org/sites/default/files/wcmsp5/groups/public/@ed_norm/@relconf/documents/meetingdocument/wcms_909906.pdf.

8. Tyler Tappendorf et al., *Improving Digital Livelihood Opportunities for Refugees: Using Community-Based Workshops to Co-Create Solutions* (UNHCR, 2023), 31, https://www.unhcr.org/innovation/wp-content/uploads/2024/02/ImprovingDigitalLivelihoodOpportunitiesforRefugees.pdf.

9. UNHCR, "UNHCR Refugee Data Finder."

10. ILO, *World Employment and Social Outlook: The Role of Digital Labour Platforms in Transforming the World of Work* (Geneva: International Labour Organization, 2021), https://www.ilo.org/global/research/global-reports/weso/2021/WCMS_771749/lang--en/index.htm.

11. Mohammad Amir Anwar and Mark Graham, *The Digital Continent: Placing Africa in Planetary Networks of Work* (Oxford: Oxford University Press, 2022).

12. Fairwork, *Fairwork Cloudwork Ratings 2023: Work in the Planetary Labour Market* (Fairwork Foundation, 2023), 7, https://fair.work/wp-content/uploads/sites/17/2023/07/Fairwork-Cloudwork-Ratings-2023-Red.pdf.

13. Tappendorf et al., *Improving Digital Livelihood Opportunities for Refugees.*

14. Evan Easton-Calabria, "Livelihoods 2.0? Refugee Self-Reliance and the Digital Gig Economy," in *Refugees, Self-Reliance, Development: A Critical History* (Bristol: Bristol University Press, 2022), 162–192.

15. Phil Jones, *Work Without the Worker* (London: Verso, 2021), 13.

16. Easton-Calabria, "Livelihoods 2.0? Refugee Self-Reliance and the Digital Gig Economy."

17. Evan Easton-Calabria, *The Migrant Union: Digital Livelihoods for People on the Move* (UNDP, 2019), https://www.undp.org/publications/digital-livelihoods-people-move.

18. Rabih Shibli, Sarah Kouzi, and Brooke Atherton El-Amine, "Digital Skills Training in Lebanon: Reinforcing Resilience in a Restrictive Environment," in *Digital Refugee Livelihoods and Decent Work: Towards Inclusion in a Fairer Digital Economy*, ed. Andreas Hackl (Geneva: International Labour Organization, 2021), 28–37.

19. Faheem Hussain, "From Persecution to 'Prosperity'? Struggles, Aspirations, and Innovations among Rohingya Refugees in Digital Entrepreneurship," in *Digital Refugee Livelihoods and Decent Work: Towards Inclusion in a Fairer Digital Economy*, ed. Andreas Hackl (Geneva: International Labour Organization, 2021), 53–60; Hervé Nicolle and Jared Owuor, "Digital Access Among Refugees in East Africa: Implications for Digital Livelihoods Provision," in *Digital Refugee Livelihoods and Decent Work: Towards Inclusion in a Fairer Digital Economy*, ed. Andreas Hackl (Geneva: International Labour Organization, 2021), 46–52.

20. Emma Samman, Dina Mansour-Ille, and Abigail Hunt, "Digital Livelihoods and Decent Work: The Refugee Gig Economy in Jordan," in *Digital Refugee Livelihoods and Decent Work: Towards Inclusion in a Fairer Digital Economy*, ed. Andreas Hackl (International Labour Organization, 2021), 67–73.

21. Lorraine Charles, "Remote Online Work for Refugees: Private Sector Perceptions," in *Digital Refugee Livelihoods and Decent Work: Towards Inclusion in a Fairer Digital Economy*, ed. Andreas Hackl (International Labour Organization, 2021), 83–89.

22. Andreas Hackl, *Towards Decent Work for Young Refugees and Host Communities in the Digital Platform Economy in Africa: Kenya, Uganda, Egypt* (Geneva: International Labour Organization, 2021), https://www.ilo.org/wcmsp5/groups/public/---ed_emp/documents/publication/wcms_816539.pdf; WUSC, MCF, and Samuel Hall, *Market Assessment of Digital Employment Opportunities for Refugee Youth* (Ottawa: World University Service of Canada, 2022), https://www.samuelhall.org/publications/wusc-amp-mastercard-foundation-market-assessment-of-digital-employment-opportunities-for-refugee-youth.

23. Tappendorf et al., *Improving Digital Livelihood Opportunities for Refugees.*

24. Andreas Hackl and Watfa Najdi, "Online Work as Humanitarian Relief? The Promise and Limitations of Digital Livelihoods for Syrian Refugees and Lebanese Youth During Times of Crisis," *Environment and Planning A: Economy and Space* 56, no. 1 (2024), https://doi.org/https://doi.org/10.1177/0308518X231184470; Hannah Johnston, "In Search of Stability at a Time of Upheaval: Digital Freelancing in Venezuela," in *Digital Work in the Planetary Market*, ed. Mark Graham and Fabian Ferrari (Cambridge, MA: MIT Press, 2022), 157–174.

25. Amanda Alencar and Julia Camargo, "Spatial Imaginaries of Digital Refugee Livelihoods," *Journal of Humanitarian Affairs* 4, no. 3 (2023), https://doi.org/10.7227/JHA.093.

26. Swati Mehta Dhawan and Julie Zollmann, "Financial Inclusion or Encampment? Rethinking Digital Finance for Refugees," *Journal of Humanitarian Affairs* 4, no. 3 (2023), https://doi.org/10.7227/JHA.094.

27. Easton-Calabria, "Livelihoods 2.0? Refugee Self-Reliance and the Digital Gig Economy."

28. Charles Martin-Shields, *Urban Refugees and Digital Technology: Reshaping Social, Political, and Economic Networks*, McGill-Queen's Refugee and Forced Migration Studies (Montreal: McGill-Queen's University Press, 2024).

29. Jenny Casswell, "The Essential Role of Digital Literacy in Contexts of Forced Displacement," *Forced Migration Review*, no. 73 (2024), 23–27.

30. Kathryn McDonald, "Structural Barriers to the Digital Platform Economy for Forcibly Displaced Workers," *Forced Migration Review*, no. 73 (2024), 42–46.

31. Marie Godin, Jean-Marie Ishimwe, and Evan Easton-Calabria, "Digital Refugee Economies in Nairobi: Opportunities and Challenges," *Forced Migration Review*, no. 73 (2024), 55–58.

32. Barbara Orth, "Stratified Pathways into Platform Work: Migration Trajectories and Skills in Berlin's Gig Economy," *Environment and Planning A: Economy and Space* 56, no. 2 (2024), https://doi.org/10.1177/0308518X231191933; Niels van Doorn and Darsana Vijay, "Gig Work as Migrant Work: The Platformization of Migration Infrastructure," *Environment and Planning A: Economy and Space* 56, no. 4 (2021), https://doi.org/10.1177/0308518X211065049.

33. van Doorn and Vijay, "Gig Work as Migrant Work: The Platformization of Migration Infrastructure."

34. ILO, *Realizing Decent Work in the Platform Economy*.

35. UNHCR, *Digital Transformation Strategy 2022–2026* (UNHCR, 2022), https://www.unhcr.org/digitalstrategy/wp-content/uploads/sites/161/2023/07/Digital-Transformation-Strategy-2022-2026-UNHCR-Web.pdf.

36. Hackl, *Towards Decent Work for Young Refugees*; UNCDF, *Inclusive Digital Economy Scorecard (IDES) Report—Uganda* (UNCDF, 2021), https://www.uncdf.org/article/7166/inclusive-digital-economy-scorecard-ides-report-uganda-2021.

37. UNCDF, "Inclusive Digital Economy Scorecard, Ethiopia," accessed November 8, 2022, https://ides.uncdf.org/2021/ETH.

38. Hussain, "From Persecution to 'Prosperity'?"

39. IFC, *Barriers and Opportunities to Refugee Women Engaging in the Digital Economy in Jordan and Lebanon* (International Finance Corporation, 2021), https://documents.worldbank.org/en/publication/documents-reports/documentdetail/759521634307903546/barriers-and-opportunities-to-refugee-women-engaging-in-the-digital-economy-in-jordan-and-lebanon-final-report; Lorraine Charles, "The Remote Work Loophole for Refugees in Jordan," *LSE Blogs*, 2022, https://blogs.lse.ac.uk/mec/2022/02/03/the-remote-work-loophole-for-refugees-in-jordan-an-incentive-towards-digital-skills-training/.

40. Hackl, *Towards Decent Work for Young Refugees*.

41. "State of Palestine: Enhancing Self-Employment of Refugees and Youth in Gaza Through Digital Channels," accessed July 30, 2024, https://open.intracen.org/projects/XM-DAC-45001-C055.

42. Tappendorf et al., *Improving Digital Livelihood Opportunities for Refugees*.

43. Easton-Calabria, *The Migrant Union*.

44. Andreas Hackl, "Connecting Without Protecting: Intermediating the Internet Economy in Digital Livelihoods Provision for Refugees," *Journal of Humanitarian Affairs* 4, no. 3 (2023), https://doi.org/10.7227/JHA.092.

45. ILO, *Realizing Decent Work in the Platform Economy*, 26.

46. "More Than 60 Per Cent of the World's Employed Population Are in the Informal Economy," accessed July 30, 2024, https://www.ilo.org/resource/news/more-60-cent-worlds-employed-population-are-informal-economy.

47. UNHCR, *Refugees' Access to Jobs and Financial Services: Background Guide Challenge Topic #3*, 2023, https://www.unhcr.org/sites/default/files/2023-03/background-guide-challenge-3-refugees-access-to-jobs-and-financial-services.pdf.

48. UNHCR, *Refugees' Access to Jobs and Financial Services.*

49. Philip Rushworth and Andreas Hackl, "Writing Code, Decoding Culture: Digital Skills and the Promise of a Fast Lane to Decent Work Among Refugees and Migrants in Berlin," *Journal of Ethnic and Migration Studies* 48, no. 11 (2021), https://doi.org/10.1080/1369183X.2021.1893159.

50. ILO, *Realizing Decent Work in the Platform Economy*, 28.

51. Elliott Prasse-Freeman, "Nothing to Lose but Their (Block)Chains," *American Ethnologist* 49, no. 4 (2022), https://doi.org/https://doi.org/10.1111/amet.13100.

52. ITU, *Facts and Figures 2021: 2.9 Billion People Still Offline* (International Telecommunications Union, 2021), https://www.itu.int/hub/2021/11/facts-and-figures-2021-2-9-billion-people-still-offline/; ITU, *Measuring Digital Development: Facts and Figures 2023* (2023), https://www.itu.int/hub/publication/d-ind-ict_mdd-2023-1/; ITU, *Measuring Digital Development: Facts and Figures 2023.*

53. Jan Van Dijk, *The Digital Divide* (Cambridge: Polity Press, 2020).

54. Hackl, *Towards Decent Work for Young Refugees.*

55. ITU, *Global Connectivity Report 2022* (International Telecommunication Union, 2022), https://www.itu.int/hub/publication/d-ind-global-01-2022/.

56. Hackl, *Towards Decent Work for Young Refugees.*

57. ILO, *World Employment and Social Outlook*, 141.

58. "Online Labour Index 2020: Online Labour Supply," Oxford Internet Institute, International Labour Organization, 2020, accessed February 20, 2023, http://onlinelabourobservatory.org/oli-supply/.

59. "The Online Labour Index 2020: Online Labour Demand," Oxford Internet Institute International Labour Organization, accessed March 20, 2023, http://onlinelabourobservatory.org/oli-demand/.

60. Fairwork, *Fairwork Cloudwork Ratings 2023*, 19–20.

61. Jones, *Work Without the Worker*, 40.

62. The Economist, "AI Firms Will Soon Exhaust Most of the Internet's Data," *The Economist*, July 23, 2024, https://www.economist.com/schools-brief/2024/07/23/ai-firms-will-soon-exhaust-most-of-the-internets-data.

63. Wiley, *Digital Skills Gap Index 2021* (2021), 14, https://dsgi.wiley.com/wp-content/uploads/2021/10/DSGI-whitepaper.pdf.

64. UNESCO, *Syrian Refugee Youth Literacy Assessment Study* (Beirut: UNESCO Regional Bureau for Education in the Arab States, 2020), 39, https://unesdoc.unesco.org/ark:/48223/pf0000375436?posInSet=231&queryId=N-469c3ef7-7963-4f86-a70b-3be43dbd5060.

65. Richard Heeks, "Digital Inequality Beyond the Digital Divide: Conceptualizing Adverse Digital Incorporation in the Global South," *Information Technology for Development* 28, no. 4 (2022), https://doi.org/10.1080/02681102.2022.2068492.

66. Dhawan and Zollmann, "Financial Inclusion or Encampment?"

67. Dhawan and Zollmann, "Financial Inclusion or Encampment?"

68. Randolph Starn, *Contrary Commonwealth: The Theme of Exile in Medieval and Renaissance Italy* (Berkeley, Los Angeles, London: University of California Press, 1982).

69. Andreas Hackl, "Key Figure of Mobility: The Exile," *Social Anthropology* 25, no. 1 (2017), 65, https://doi.org/10.1111/1469-8676.12380.

70. Mark Graham and Fabian Ferrari, "Introduction," in *Digital Work in the Planetary Market*, ed. Mark Graham and Fabian Ferrari (The MIT Press, 2022), 8.

71. Edward Said, "Reflections on Exile," in *Reflections on Exile: And Other Literary and Cultural Essays* (London: Granta, 2001), 185.

72. Said, "Reflections on Exile," 177.

73. Hackl, "Key Figure of Mobility: The Exile," 57.

74. "Digital Transformation in Ukraine: Before, During, and After the War," accessed August 20, 2025, https://www.sir.advancedleadership.harvard.edu/articles/digital-transformation-in-ukraine-before-during-after-war.

75. Ana Paula Cusolito et al., *The Upside of Digital for the Middle East and North Africa: How Digital Technology Adoption Can Accelerate Growth and Create Jobs*, (World Bank, 2021), https://openknowledge.worldbank.org/bitstream/handle/10986/37058/9781464816635.pdf?sequence=10&isAllowed=y.

76. Andreas Hackl, "Digital Livelihoods in Exile: Refugee Work and the Planetary Digital Labor Market," in *Digital Work in the Planetary Market*, ed. Mark Graham and Fabian Ferrari (Cambridge, MA: MIT Press, 2022); Anwar and Graham, *The Digital Continent*.

77. Heeks, "Digital Inequality Beyond the Digital Divide: Conceptualizing Adverse Digital Incorporation in the Global South."

Chapter 1

* This chapter is in part derived from an article published in the journal *Environment and Planning A: Economy and Space* (2023, vol. 56, no. 1), published Open Access under Creative Commons License (CC BY 4.0) by Sage, and available online at https://doi.org/10.1177/0308518X231184470.

1. World Bank, *Lebanon Economic Monitor: Lebanon Sinking (To the Top 3)* (2021), https://documents1.worldbank.org/curated/en/394741622469174252/pdf/Lebanon-Economic-Monitor-Lebanon-Sinking-to-the-Top-3.pdf.

2. UNHCR, WFP, and UNICEF, *Vulnerability Assessment of Syrian Refugees in Lebanon* (2016), https://ialebanon.unhcr.org/vasyr/files/vasyr_reports/vasyr-2016.pdf.

3. Vili Lehdonvirta, "Algorithms That Divide and Unite: Delocalisation, Identity and Collective Action in 'Microwork,'" in *Space, Place and Global Digital Work. Dynamics of Virtual Work*, ed. J. Flecker (London: Palgrave Macmillan, 2016), 53–80.

4. UNHCR, UNICEF, and WFP, *VASyR 2019: Vulnerability Assessment of Syrian Refugees in Lebanon* (2019), 10.

5. ILO, *World Employment and Social Outlook*.

6. Stephany, Kässi, and Lehdonvirta, "The Online Labour Index 2020: Online Labour Demand."

7. Shibli, Kouzi, and Atherton El-Amine, "Digital Skills Training in Lebanon."

8. UNHCR, UNICEF, and WFP, *VASyR 2019*, 10–11.

9. UNHCR, UNICEF, and WFP, *VASyR 2019*, 11–12.

10. Maysa Baroud and Nour Zeidan, *Addressing Challenges Faced by Syrian Refugees Working in the Informal Economy: Case Studies from Lebanon and Jordan* (Issam Fares Institute of Public Policy and International Affairs, American University of Beirut: 2021), https://www.aub.edu.lb/ifi/Documents/publications/policy_briefs/2020-20/20210101_addressing_challenges_faced_by_syrian_refugees_brief.pdf.

11. ILO PROSPECTS, *Review of National Policy, Legislative and Regulatory Frameworks and Practice: A Baseline Study on the Right to Work and Rights at Work for Refugees*

(International Labour Office: Geneva, 2023), https://www.ilo.org/wcmsp5/groups/public/---dgreports/---ddg_p/documents/publication/wcms_882697.pdf.

12. ILO PROSPECTS, *Review of National Policy.*

13. LEADERS, *The Labour Sector in Lebanon: Legal Frameworks, Challenges, and Opportunities* (LEADERS for Sustainable Livelihoods: 2019), 35, https://reliefweb.int/attachments/7f314e73-7413-33a7-9d02-dc681d64d219/69776.pdf.

14. Inter-Agency Coordination Lebanon and UNDP, *Questions & Answers for LCRP Partners: Recent Demonstrations and Municipal Restrictions Against Syrian Refugees Labour Competition and Businesses, Lebanon* (2017), https://reliefweb.int/report/lebanon/questions-answers-lcrp-partners-recent-demonstrations-and-municipal-restrictions.

15. Easton-Calabria, *The Migrant Union.*

16. Lily C. Irani and M. Six Silberman, "Turkopticon: Interrupting Worker Invisibility in Amazon Mechanical Turk," *Proceedings of the SIGCHI Conference on . . .* (2013), https://doi.org/10.1145/2470654.2470742.

17. Adam Fejerskov, *The Global Lab: Inequality, Technology, and the Experimental Movement* (Oxford: Oxford University Press, 2022).

18. Dina Mansour-Ille and Demi Starks, "Breaking Barriers: Digital Work and Fragile Livelihoods of Women Refugees in the Middle East and North Africa," *Journal of Humanitarian Affairs* 4, no. 3 (2023), https://doi.org/10.7227/JHA.096.

19. Shibli, Kouzi, and Atherton El-Amine, "Digital Skills Training in Lebanon," 32.

20. Kawthar Dara, *Marginalization Cost: Regional Disparities Fueling Lebanon's Fragility* (Washington, DC: Carnegie Endowment for International Peace, 2020), https://carnegieendowment.org/files/Dara_Spatial_inequalities.pdf.

21. Freedom House, *Freedom on the Net 2021: Lebanon* (Washington, DC: Freedom House, 2021), https://freedomhouse.org/country/lebanon/freedom-net/2021.

22. ILO, *Assessing Informality and Vulnerability Among Disadvantaged Groups in Lebanon: A Survey of Lebanese, and Syrian and Palestinian Refugees* (Geneva: International Labour Organizaton 2021), https://www.ilo.org/beirut/media-centre/news/WCMS_818370/lang--en/index.htm.

23. Zoe Hamilton, Matthew Downer, and Susanna Acland, *The Digital Worlds of Displacement-Affected Communities: A Cross-Context Study of How People Affected by Displacement Use Mobile Phones* (London: GSMA, 2022), 19, https://www.gsma.com/mobilefordevelopment/wp-content/uploads/2022/10/DigitalWorldsDAC_R2_WEB.pdf.

24. "ITU DataHub: Data-Only Mobile Broadband Basket," accessed July 5, 2024, https://datahub.itu.int/data/?i=34617&e=LBN.

25. Clément Gibon, "24-Carat 4G: In Crisis-Hit Lebanon, Mobile Phones and Broadband Are Now Only for the Rich," *The New Arab*, July 6, 2022, https://www.newarab.com/features/crisis-hit-lebanon-mobile-and-broadband-are-rich.

26. Hamilton, Downer, and Acland, *The Digital Worlds of Displacement-Affected Communities: A Cross-Context Study of How People Affected by Displacement Use Mobile Phones*, 17.

27. ITU, *Measuring Digital Development. Facts and Figures: Focus on Least Developed Countries* (Geneva: International Telecommunications Union, 2023), https://www.itu.int/hub/publication/d-ind-ict_mdd-2023/.

28. UNHCR, *Displaced and Disconnected: Country Reports* (Geneva: UNHCR Innovation Service, 2022), 51, https://www.unhcr.org/innovation/wp-content/uploads/2022/03/Displaced-and-Disconnected-Country-Reports-ENGLISH.pdf.

29. Chloe Domat, "Show Me the Money! No Bank Accounts for Many Syrians in Lebanon," *Middle East Eye*, December 19, 2016, https://www.middleeasteye.net/features/show-me-money-no-bank-accounts-many-syrians-lebanon.

30. Andreas Hackl and Margie Cheesman, *The Identity Issue: Digital Risks of Proxy IDs in Kenya's Online Economy* (UNHCR Innovation Service, 2023), https://medium.com/unhcr-innovation-service/the-identity-issue-digital-risks-of-proxy-ids-in-kenyas-digital-economy-52eec129ebea.

31. ILO, *World Employment and Social Outlook*, 93.

32. Wala Mohammed, "The Digital Exclusion of Refugees and IDPs in Sudan," *Forced Migration Review* 73 (2024), https://www.fmreview.org/digital-disruption/mohammed/.

33. "ID Verification Syria Is Not Listed," accessed July 5, 2024, https://community.upwork.com/t5/New-to-Upwork/Re-ID-verification-Syria-is-not-listed/m-p/549134.

34. Hackl, "Digital Livelihoods in Exile."

35. World Bank, *Lebanon Poverty and Equity Assessment 2024: Weathering a Protracted Crisis* (Washington, DC: The World Bank, 2024), https://documents1.worldbank.org/curated/en/099052224104516741/pdf/P1766511325da10a71ab6b1ae97816dd20c.pdf.

36. CAS and ILO, *Lebanon Follow-Up Labour Force Survey: January 2022* (Beirut: International Labour Organization and Central Administration of Statistics Lebanon, 2022), https://www.ilo.org/wcmsp5/groups/public/---arabstates/---ro-beirut/documents/publication/wcms_848353.pdf; ILO, *Assessing Informality and Vulnerability among Disadvantaged Groups in Lebanon*.

37. World Bank, "Lebanon's Fragile Economy Pulled Back into Recession," news release, December 21, 2023, https://www.worldbank.org/en/news/press-release/2023

/12/21/lebanon-s-fragile-economy-pulled-back-into-recession#:~:text=With%20the%20onset%20of%20the,of%2012.8%20percent%20of%20GDP.

38. ILO, *World Employment and Social Outlook*, 44.

39. "Online Labour Index 'Online Labour Supply,'" Online Labour Observatory, accessed May 25, 2023, http://onlinelabourobservatory.org/oli-supply/.

40. OMSAR, *Lebanon Digital Transformation: National Strategy May 2022 Update* (Beirut: Republic of Lebanon Office of the Minister of State for Administrative Reform, 2022), https://omsar.gov.lb/Assets/DT_EN.pdf.

41. "Lebanon's Internet Could Go Dark Amid Strike by State-Owned Ogero's Workers," accessed July 5, 2025, https://www.thenationalnews.com/mena/lebanon/2023/03/24/workers-of-lebanons-state-owned-telco-ogero-begin-indefinite-strike/.

42. OMSAR, *Lebanon Digital Transformation*, 39.

43. ILO, *World Employment and Social Outlook*, 141.

44. Kawthar Dara, "Peripheries of Poverty: In an Interview, Kawthar Dara Discusses How Regional Disparities Have Added to Lebanon's Fragility," interview by Michael Young, September 29, 2020.

45. "A Financial Crisis, Then Coronavirus. Lebanese Universities Could Still Thrive," Al-Fanar Media, 2020, accessed May 8, 2021, https://www.al-fanarmedia.org/2020/03/a-financial-crisis-then-coronavirus-lebanese-universities-could-still-thrive/.

46. Hana Addam El-Ghali and Fida Alameddine, *Syrian Refugee Students in Lebanese Higher Education: Recognition of Qualifications and Beyond* (Beirut: Issam Fares Institute for Public Policy and International Affairs, 2019), https://www.aub.edu.lb/ifi/Documents/publications/research_reports/2019-2020/20190107_syrian_refugee_students_in_lebanese_higher_education.pdf.

47. Johnston, "In Search of Stability at a Time of Upheaval."

48. Reuters, "Lebanon Currency Drops to New Low as Financial Meltdown Deepens," June 13, 2021, https://www.reuters.com/world/middle-east/lebanon-currency-drops-new-low-financial-meltdown-deepens-2021-06-13/.

49. Louise Brosset, "What Digital Services to Pay Forcibly Displaced Persons Remotely in Lebanon and Increase Financial Inclusion?" Techfugees, 2021, accessed August 20, 2022, https://techfugees.com/all_news/what-digital-services-to-pay-forcibly-displaced-persons-remotely-in-lebanon-and-increase-financial-inclusion/.

50. Reuters, *Lebanon C. Bank Sets New Rate for Withdrawals from Dollar Deposits*, January 2, 2023, https://www.reuters.com/business/finance/lebanon-cbank-sets-new-rate-withdrawals-dollar-deposits-2023-01-20/.

51. AP, "Lebanon Sets New Exchange Rate, Dramatically Devalues Pound," *Associated Press*, February 1, 2023, https://apnews.com/article/inflation-international-monetary-fund-beirut-lebanon-business-6f7fb7e8bfa93ca23e6caaf47a61f8d7.

52. Ricardo Hausmann et al., *Towards a Sustainable Recovery for Lebanon's Economy*, CID Faculty Working Paper No. 439 (Cambridge, MA: Centre for International Development at Harvard University and Growth Lab, 2023), http://www.tinyurl.com/ywjtpnhg.

53. Alawsat Asharq, "Employees in Lebanon Earn Among Lowest Salaries Worldwide," Asharq Alawsat Online, February 26, 2021, https://english.aawsat.com/home/article/2828886/employees-lebanon-earn-among-lowest-salaries-worldwide.

54. Johnston, "In Search of Stability at a Time of Upheaval," 166.

55. Shibli, Kouzi, and Atherton El-Amine, "Digital Skills Training in Lebanon."

56. Shibli, Kouzi, and Atherton El-Amine, "Digital Skills Training in Lebanon," 32.

57. "NaTakallam: Our Story," accessed February 20, 2025, https://natakallam.com/about/.

58. John Bryant, *Digital Technologies and Inclusion in Humanitarian Response* (London: Overseas Development Institute, 2022), https://media.odi.org/documents/Digital_inclusion_synthesis.pdf.

59. Peter Redfield, *Life in Crisis: The Ethical Journey of Doctors Without Borders* (Berkeley, Los Angeles, London: University of California Press, 2013), 14.

60. Hackl, "Key Figure of Mobility," 64–65.

61. Kassem Mnejja, *Israel's Digital Assault on Lebanon* (Washington, DC: The Tahrir Institute for Middle East Policy, 2024), https://timep.org/2024/12/04/israels-digital-assault-on-lebanon/.

62. AFP, "Lebanon's Mikati Calls on Syrians to Return Home," France24, December 14, 2024, https://www.france24.com/en/live-news/20241214-lebanon-s-mikati-calls-on-syrians-to-return-home.

63. "Access Now Demands U.S. Lift Sanctions Blocking Syria's Digital Recovery," Access Now, updated January 31, 2025, accessed February 22, 2025, https://www.accessnow.org/press-release/open-letter-us-lift-syria-sanctions/.

Chapter 2

1. IFC and Google, *E-Conomy Africa 2020: Africa's $180 Billion Internet Economy Future* (Wasington, DC: International Finance Corporation and Google, 2020), https://www.ifc.org/wps/wcm/connect/e358c23f-afe3-49c5-a509-034257688580/e-Conomy-Africa-2020.pdf?MOD=AJPERES&CVID=nmuGYF2.

2. Kutoma J. Wakunuma and Tom Kwanya, "Towards a Socially Just Gig Economy in Kenya: Stakeholder Engagement and Regulatory Processes," *Digital Society Blog, The Humboldt Institute for Internet and Society*, 2023, https://www.hiig.de/en/socially-just-gig-economy-kenya/.

3. "Ajira Digital Program and Amahoro Coalition Collaborate to Enable Online Work for Refugees," KEPSA, 2022, accessed July 4, 2024, https://kepsa.or.ke/kepsanews/ajira-digital-program-and-amahoro-coalition-collaborate-to-enable-online-work-for-refugees.

4. "Online Labour Index: Online Labour Supply," accessed January 27, 2025, http://onlinelabourobservatory.org/oli-supply/.

5. ILO, *Digital Labour Platforms in Kenya: Exploring Women's Opportunities and Challenges across Various Sectors* (Geneva: International Labour Organization, 2024), 148, https://www.ilo.org/wcmsp5/groups/public/---dgreports/---ddg_p/documents/publication/wcms_920520.pdf.

6. ILO, *Digital Labour Platforms in Kenya*, 19.

7. ILO, *Digital Labour Platforms in Kenya*.

8. Heeks, "Digital Inequality Beyond the Digital Divide."

9. "Refugees and Asylum Seekers in Kenya," 2025, accessed March 30, 2025, https://data.unhcr.org/en/country/ken.

10. ILO, *Review of National Policy, Legislative and Regulatory Frameworks and Practice in Kenya: A Baseline Study on the Right to Work and Rights at Work for Refugees* (Geneva: International Labour Organization, 2022), xii, https://www.ilo.org/wcmsp5/groups/public/---dgreports/---ddg_p/documents/publication/wcms_864207.pdf.

11. Foni Joyce Vuni and Buhendwa Iragi, *Refugees' Access to Work Permits and Business Licenses in Kenya*, Refugee-Led Research Series, Research Report 7 (Nairobi: British Institute in East Africa, 2023), https://drive.google.com/file/d/1exbrWY7rzXvXtECkNkyZSIrY8w8T7oth/view.

12. ILO, *Review of National Policy, Legislative and Regulatory Frameworks and Practice in Kenya*, xii.

13. NRC, *Access to Movement Passes: A Roadmap to Self-Reliance for Refugee Entrepreneurs in Dadaab* (Norwegian Refugee Council, 2022), https://www.nrc.no/globalassets/pdf/briefing-notes/kakumas-refugees-freedom-of-movement/access-to-movement-passes---self-reliance-of-entrepreneurs-in-dadaab.pdf.

14. ILO, *Review of National Policy, Legislative and Regulatory Frameworks and Practice in Kenya*, 30.

15. Alexander Betts et al., "The Economic Lives of Refugees," *World Development* 182 (2024), https://doi.org/https://doi.org/10.1016/j.worlddev.2024.106693.

16. Betts et al., "The Economic Lives of Refugees."

17. Nicolas Friederici, Michael Wahome, and Mark Graham, *Digital Entrepreneurship in Africa: How a Continent Is Escaping Silicon Valley's Long Shadow* (Cambridge, MA: MIT Press, 2019).

18. Republic of Kenya, *Digital Economy Blueprint: Powering Kenya's Transformation* (2019), 7, 18, https://smartafrica.org/wp-content/uploads/2021/08/Kenya_Digital_Economy_2019.pdf.

19. ITU, *Measuring Digital Development.*

20. ITU, *Measuring Digital Development.*

21. Tappendorf et al., *Improving Digital Livelihood Opportunities for Refugees*, 123.

22. Republic of Kenya, *Digital Economy Blueprint.*

23. Republic of Kenya, *The Kenya National Digital Master Plan: 2022–2032*, 50–4.

24. GSMA, *Mobile Taxation in Kenya: Accelerating Digital Development* (GSMA and EY, 2020), 25–31.

25. "Inability to Provide Tax Information on Upwork Due to Lack of KRA Pin for Refugees," Upwork Community Forum, 2024, accessed August 12, 2024, https://community.upwork.com/t5/Freelancers/Inability-to-Provide-Tax-Information-on-Upwork-Due-to-Lack-of/td-p/1502288.

26. Fairwork, *Fairwork Kenya Ratings 2021: Labour Standards in the Gig Economy* (Fairwork Foundation, 2021), 50, https://fair.work/wp-content/uploads/sites/17/2021/12/Fairwork-Kenya-2021-Report.pdf.

27. Billy Perrigo, "Inside Facebook's African Sweatshop," *Time*, February 14, 2022, https://time.com/6147458/facebook-africa-content-moderation-employee-treatment/.

28. Caroline Kimeu, "High-Profile Lawsuit Against Meta Can Be Heard in Kenya, Nairobi Court Rules," *The Guardian*, February 7, 2023, https://www.theguardian.com/global-development/2023/feb/07/lawsuit-meta-kenya-nairobi-court-rules-facebook-ptsd.

29. The Economist, "Three Big Lawsuits Against Meta in Kenya May Have Global Implications," *The Economist*, January 23, 2025, https://www.economist.com/middle-east-and-africa/2025/01/23/three-big-lawsuits-against-meta-in-kenya-may-have-global-implications.

30. AP, "Kenya-Based Content Moderators Mourn Nigerian Colleague Who 'Was Desperate to Go Home,'" *Associated Press*, March 12, 2025, https://apnews.com/article/kenya-content-moderators-facebook-tik-tok-aa8cd8bd993c38d4701a64cfb7cd8ee6.

31. ILO and FKE, *The Informal Economy in Kenya* (Nairobi: International Labour Organization, Federation of Kenya Employers, 2021), https://www.ilo.org/wcmsp5/groups/public/---ed_emp/---emp_ent/documents/publication/wcms_820312.pdf.

32. Fairwork, *Fairwork Kenya Ratings 2021: Labour Standards in the Gig Economy*, 21.

33. ILO, *Digital Labour Platforms in Kenya*, 145.

34. Meghan E. Ference, Tatiana Thieme, and Naomi van Stapele, "Harnessing the 'Hustle': Struggle, Solidarities and Narratives of Work in Nairobi and Beyond Introduction," *Africa* 91, no. 1 (2021), https://doi.org/10.1017/S0001972020000819.

35. Brian Ekdale and Ebenezer Aidoo, "Navigating Platform Work Through Solidarity and Hustling: The Case of Ride-Hailing Drivers in Nairobi, Kenya," *Online Media and Global Communication* 3, no. 3 (2024), https://doi.org/10.1515/omgc-2024-0017.

36. Andrew Leon Hanna, *25 Million Sparks: The Untold Story of Refugee Entrepreneurs* (Cambridge: Cambridge University Press, 2022), 93.

37. ILO, *Digital Labour Platforms in Kenya*, 145.

38. ILO, *Digital Labour Platforms in Kenya*, xvi.

39. Sonia Gomez et al., "Education as a Catalyst for Refugee and Host Community Integration in Kenya," UNHCR, December 12, 2024, https://www.unhcr.org/blogs/education-as-a-catalyst-for-refugee-and-host-community-integration-in-kenya/#:~:text=In%20refugee%20camps%20like%20Kakuma,among%20hosts%20in%20urban%20areas.

40. Betts et al., "The Economic Lives of Refugees."

41. KEPSA, "Ajira Digital Program and Amahoro Coalition Collaborate to Enable Online Work for Refugees."

42. Interview, Halkano Boru, ITC, August 26, 2022; ILO, "Digitally Empowering Young People in Refugee and Host Communities. What Is Possible? A Mapping Study in Kenya," 2021. https://www.ilo.org/wcmsp5/groups/public/---dgreports/---ddg_p/documents/publication/wcms_810061.pdf.

43. WUSC, MCF, and Samuel Hall, *Market Assessment of Digital Employment Opportunities for Refugee Youth*.

44. WUSC, MCF, and Samuel Hall, *Market Assessment of Digital Employment Opportunities for Refugee Youth*, 41.

45. Samuel Hall, Elrha, and HIF, *Innovating Mobile Solutions for Refugees in East Africa: Opportunities and Barrier to Using Mobile Technology and the Internet in Kakuma Refugee Camp and Nakivale Refugee Settlement* (Samuel Hall, Elrha, HIF, 2018), 18–19, https://www.elrha.org/wp-content/uploads/2018/02/Innovating_mobile_soultions_Report.pdf.

46. Godin, Ishimwe, and Easton-Calabria, "Digital Refugee Economies in Nairobi."

47. ITU, *Global Connectivity Report 2022*, 25.

48. GSMA, *The Mobile Gender Gap Report 2023* (GSMA, 2023), 17, https://www.gsma.com/r/wp-content/uploads/2023/06/The-Mobile-Gender-Gap-Report-2023.pdf?utm_source=website&utm_medium=download-button&utm_campaign=gender-gap-2023.

49. GSMA, *The Mobile Gender Gap Report 2023*, 14–15.

50. WUSC, MCF, and Samuel Hall, *Market Assessment of Digital Employment Opportunities for Refugee Youth.*

51. Tappendorf et al., *Improving Digital Livelihood Opportunities for Refugees*, 123.

52. Stephen Okello, *The Energy Situation in the Dadaab Refugee Camps, Kenya*, Research Paper (London: The Royal Institute of International Affairs, 2016), https://www.chathamhouse.org/sites/default/files/publications/research/2016-05-19-mei-energy-situation-dadaab-refugee-camps-okello-final.pdf.

53. ILO, *Digital Labour Platforms in Kenya*, xviii.

54. ILO, *Digital Labour Platforms in Kenya*, xvii.

55. WUSC, MCF, and Samuel Hall, *Market Assessment of Digital Employment Opportunities for Refugee Youth*, 17.

56. WUSC, MCF, and Samuel Hall, *Market Assessment of Digital Employment Opportunities for Refugee Youth*, 17.

57. Heeks, "Digital Inequality Beyond the Digital Divide."

58. Aaron Martin, *Connecting with Confidence: Managing Digital Risks to Refugee Connectivity*, (Geneva: UNHCR, 2021), 30, https://www.unhcr.org/innovation/wp-content/uploads/2021/03/CWC-Managing-Digital-Risks-To-Refugee-Connectivity-Report.pdf.

59. Jo Burton, "'Doing No Harm' in the Digital Age: What the Digitalization of Cash Means for Humanitarian Action," *International Review of the Red Cross* 102, no. 913 (2020), https://doi.org/10.1017/S1816383120000491.

60. Hackl, "Connecting Without Protecting."

61. ILO, *Review of National Policy, Legislative and Regulatory Frameworks and Practice in Kenya*, 30.

62. UNHCR, *Displaced and Disconnected: East and Horn of Africa and Great Lakes Region* (Geneva: UNHCR Innovation Service, 2022), 5, https://www.unhcr.org/innovation/wp-content/uploads/2023/02/Displaced-and-Disconnected-East-Africa-1.pdf

63. "How to Get a Kenya Revenue Authority Personal Identification Number (KRA PIN) for an Individual—A Guide for Refugees in Kenya," 2022, accessed February 2, 2023, https://www.julisha.info/hc/en-us/articles/4414154969751-How-to-get-a-Kenya-Revenue-Authority-Personal-Identification-Number-KRA-PIN-for-an-individual-A-guide-for-refugees-in-Kenya-.

64. UNHCR, *Displaced and Disconnected: East and Horn of Africa and Great Lakes Region*, 3–4.

65. Tavneet Suri and William Jack, "The Long-Run Poverty and Gender Impacts of Mobile Money," *Science* 354, no. 6317 (2016), https://doi.org/10.1126/science.aah5309.

66. UNHCR, *Displaced and Disconnected.*

67. UNHCR, *Displaced and Disconnected.*

68. Alexander Betts, Naohiko Omata, and Olivier Sterck, *Refugee Economies in Kenya* (Oxford: 2020).

69. ILO, *Digital Labour Platforms in Kenya*, xix.

70. WUSC, MCF, and Samuel Hall, *Market Assessment of Digital Employment Opportunities for Refugee Youth*, 17.

71. Heeks, "Digital Inequality Beyond the Digital Divide."

72. Graham and Ferrari, "Introduction," 4.

Chapter 3

* This chapter is in part derived from an article in the *Journal of Ethnic and Migration Studies* (2022, vol. 48, no. 11), published by Taylor & Francis, available online at https://doi.org/10.1080/1369183X.2021.1893159.

1. "We're All Part of the Problem," The State of European Tech, 2018, https://2018.stateofeuropeantech.com/chapter/diversity-inclusion/article/were-all-part-problem/, accessed October 5, 2020.

2. Melissa Gregg, "Hack for Good: Speculative Labour, App Development and the Burden of Austerity," *The Fibreculture Journal* 25 (2015), https://twentyfive.fibreculturejournal.org.

3. Ben Mason, *Tech Jobs for Refugees: Assessing the Potential of Coding Schools for Refugee Integration in Germany* (Brussels: Migration Policy Institute, 2018), https://www.bosch-stiftung.de/sites/default/files/publications/pdf/2018-11/TechJobsRefugees_Final.pdf.

4. Alexandra Embiricos, "From Refugee to Entrepreneur? Challenges to Refugee Self-Reliance in Berlin, Germany," *Journal of Refugee Studies* 33, no. 1 (2020), https://doi.org/10.1093/jrs/fez073.

5. Ben Mason, Lavinia Schwedersky, and Akram Alfawakheeri, *Digital Routes to Integration-How Civic Tech Innovations Are Supporting Refugees in Germany* (Berlin: Betterplace Lab, 2017), https://www.betterplace-lab.org/en/digitale-wege-zur-integration.

6. Evan Easton-Calabria and Jennifer Wood, "Bridging, Bonding, and Linking? Syrian Refugee-led Organisations and Integration in Berlin," *Journal of Ethnic and Migration Studies* 47, no. 19 (2020), https://doi.org/10.1080/1369183X.2020.1788928.

7. Gracia Liu-Farrer and Karen Shire, "Who Are the fittest? The Question of Skills in National Employment Systems in an Age of Global Labour Mobility," *Journal of Ethnic and Migration Studies* 47, no. 10 (2021): 2, https://doi.org/10.1080/1369183X.2020.1731987.

8. van Doorn and Vijay, "Gig Work as Migrant Work."

9. "5 Reasons to Work in the IT Sector in Germany," https://www.make-it-in-germany.com/en/working-in-germany/it-specialist-in-germany/work-in-it.

10. Clive Thompson, *Coders: Who They Are, What They Think and How They Are Changing Our World* (London: Picador, 2019), 99.

11. Stef Jansen, "Misplaced Masculinities: Status Loss and the Location of Gendered Subjectivities Amongst 'Non-Transnational' Bosnian Refugees," *Anthropological Theory* 8, no. 2 (2008), https://doi.org/10.1177/1463499608090790.

12. Brooke Erin Duffy, "The Romance of Work: Gender and Aspirational Labour in the Digital Culture Industries," *International Journal of Cultural Studies* 19, no. 4 (2015), https://doi.org/10.1177/1367877915572186.

13. Sophie Hinger, "Integration Through Disintegration? The Distinction Between Deserving and Undeserving Refugees in National and Local Integration Policies in Germany," in *Politics of (Dis)Integration*, ed. Sophie Hinger and Reinhard Schweitzer (Cham: Springer Open, 2020), 27.

14. Bundesagentur für Arbeit, *Fluchtmigration* (Nürnberg, 2020).

15. OECD, "Migration Snapshot of the City of Berlin," in *Working Together for Local Integration of Migrants and Refugees in Berlin* (Paris: OECD, 2018), 28.

16. "Skilled Personnel Welcome: A New Law Faciliates the Migration of Skilled Workers to Germany. Here Are the Requirements," Deutschland.de, 2020, accessed July 23, 2022, https://www.deutschland.de/en/topic/business/the-skilled-labour-immigration-act-working-in-germany.

17. "Germany: New 'Skilled Workers Immigration Act' Enacted," Library of Congress, 2023, accessed July 10, 2024, https://www.loc.gov/item/global-legal-monitor/2023-08-24/germany-new-skilled-workers-immigration-act-enacted/.

18. OECD, "Migration Snapshot of the City of Berlin."

19. Manfred Kühn, "Immigration Strategies of Cities: Local Growth Policies and Urban Planning in Germany," *European Planning Studies* 26, no. 9 (2018), https://doi.org/10.1080/09654313.2018.1484428; Hinger, "Integration Through Disintegration?"

20. OECD, "Migration Snapshot of the City of Berlin."

21. Bundesagentur für Arbeit, *Fluchtmigration*.

22. Bundesagentur für Arbeit, "Personen im Kontext von Fluchtmigration (Monatszahlen). Juni 2024," 2024, https://statistik.arbeitsagentur.de/SiteGlobals/Forms/Suche/Einzelheftsuche_Formular.html?nn=20832&topic_f=fluchtkontext.

23. Xiang Biao, *Global "Body Shopping": An Indian Labor System in the Information Technology Industry* (Princeton, NJ: Princeton University Press, 2007).

24. Sareeta Amrute, *Encoding Race, Encoding Class: Indian IT Workers in Berlin* (Durham, NC: Duke University Press, 2016).

25. Amrute, "Encoding Race, Encoding Class: Indian IT Workers in Berlin," 2.

26. Morgan Etzel, "New Models of the 'Good Refugee'—Bureaucratic Expectations of Syrian Refugees in Germany," *Ethnic and Racial Studies* 45, no. 6 (2021), https://doi.org/10.1080/01419870.2021.1954679.

27. Tobias G. Eule, *Inside Immigration Law: Migration Management and Policy Application in Germany* (London: Routledge, 2016).

28. Hinger, "Integration Through Disintegration?"

29. Evan Easton-Calabria, *Refugees, Self-Reliance, Development: A Critical History*, 1st ed. (Bristol: Bristol University Press, 2022), 195.

30. Evan Easton-Calabria and Naohiko Omata, "Panacea for the Refugee Crisis? Rethinking the Promotion of 'Self-Reliance' for Refugees," *Third World Quarterly* (2018): 1462, https://doi.org/10.1080/01436597.2018.1458301.

31. "Hacking the Refugee Crisis," YouTube, 2016, accessed April 20, 2023, https://www.youtube.com/watch?v=wz0mlDELSo0.

32. Easton-Calabria, *The Migrant Union*, 20.

33. Thompson, *Coders*, 209.

34. Harald Bauder, "'Brain Abuse,' or the Devaluation of Immigrant Labour in Canada," *Antipode* 35, no. 4 (2003), https://doi.org/10.1046/j.1467-8330.2003.00346.x.

35. Duffy, "The Romance of Work."

36. Liu-Farrer and Shire, "Who Are the Fittest? The Question of Skills in National Employment Systems in an Age of Global Labour Mobility," 6.

37. Andreas Hackl, "Good Immigrants, Permitted Outsiders: Conditional Inclusion and Citizenship in Comparison," *Ethnic and Racial Studies* 45, no. 6 (2022), https://doi.org/10.1080/01419870.2021.2011938.

Chapter 4

1. UNHCR, "UNHCR Refugee Data Finder."

2. UNHCR, *Sudan: Global Apeal 2025 Situation Overview* (2025), https://reporting.unhcr.org/sites/default/files/2024-11/Sudan%20Situation%20Overview.pdf.

3. "Reported Impact Snapshot Gaza Strip (25 March, 2025)," 2025, https://www.ochaopt.org/content/reported-impact-snapshot-gaza-strip-25-march-2025.

4. "Occupied Palestinian Territory," accessed March 26, 2025, https://www.unocha.org/occupied-palestinian-territory#:~:text=Ninety%20per%20cent%20of%20Gaza's,clean%20water%2C%20education%20and%20livelihoods.

5. Ozge Demirci, Jonas Hannane, and Xinrong Zhu, "Who Is AI Replacing? The Impact of Generative AI on Online Freelancing Platforms," 2023, http://dx.doi.org/10.2139/ssrn.4602944.

6. ILO, "Changing Demand for Skills in Digital Economies and Societies: Literature Review and Case Studies from Low- and Middle-Income Countries," 2021, https://www.ilo.org/skills/areas/skills-training-for-poverty-reduction/WCMS_831372/lang--en/index.htm.

7. AP, "Kenya-Based Content Moderators Mourn Nigerian Colleague Who 'Was Desperate to Go Home,'" *Associated Press*, March 20, 2025, https://apnews.com/article/kenya-content-moderators-facebook-tik-tok-aa8cd8bd993c38d4701a64cfb7cd8ee6.

8. Heeks, "Digital Inequality Beyond the Digital Divide."

9. Dragana Kaurin, *Space and Imagination: Rethinking Refugees' Digital Access* (Geneva: UNHCR Innovation Service, 2020), 6, https://www.unhcr.org/innovation/wp-content/uploads/2020/04/Space-and-imagination-rethinking-refugees'-digital-access_WEB042020.pdf.

10. Mark Stefik, *Internet Dreams: Archetypes, Myths, and Metaphors* (Cambridge, MA: MIT Press, 2001).

11. Noel B. Salazar, "Key Figures of Mobility: An Introduction," *Social Anthropology* 25 (2017), https://doi.org/10.1111/1469-8676.12393.

12. Friederici, Wahome, and Graham, *Digital Entrepreneurship in Africa*.

13. Kaurin, *Space and Imagination*, 1.

14. Hanna, *25 Million Sparks*, 93.

15. Salazar, "Key Figures of Mobility."

16. Johan Lindquist, "Of Figures and Types: Brokering Knowledge and Migration in Indonesia and Beyond," *Journal of the Royal Anthropological Institute* 21, no. S1 (2015): 163, https://doi.org/10.1111/1467-9655.12172.

17. Andreas Hackl, *The Invisible Palestinians: The Hidden Struggle for Inclusion in Jewish Tel Aviv* (Bloomington: Indiana University Press, 2022).

18. Saskia Sassen, *The Mobility of Labor and Capital: A Study in International Investment and Labor Flow* (Cambridge: Cambridge University Press, 1988).

19. Michel Agier, *Managing the Undesirables: Refugee Camps and Humanitarian Government* (Cambridge: Polity Press, 2011).

20. Mark Graham and Mohammad Anwar, "The Global Gig Economy: Towards a Planetary Labour Market?," *First Monday* 24, no. 4 (2019), https://doi.org/10.5210/fm.v24i4.9913.

21. Michel Agier, "The Ghetto, the Hyperghetto and the Fragmentation of the World," *International Journal of Urban and Regional Research* 33, no. 3 (2009), https://doi.org/10.1111/j.1468-2427.2009.00922.x.

22. Sara Roy, *Failing Peace: Gaza and the Palestinian-Israeli Conflict* (London: Pluto Press, 2006), 2.

23. "'We Have No Choice': Gazan Workers Find a Lifeline in Freelancing Amid War," *The Guardian*, November 3, 2025, https://www.theguardian.com/world/2024/nov/03/remote-worker-gaza-palestine-israel-war.

24. Gaza Sky Geeks, *The Impact of the Gaza Crisis on the Palestinian Tech Ecosystem* (Portland, OR: Mercy Corps, 2024), https://www.mercycorps.org/sites/default/files/2024-07/gsg-report2_compressed-5.pdf.

25. Jones, *Work Without the Worker*, 13.

26. Agier, "The Ghetto, the Hyperghetto and the Fragmentation of the World."

27. Guillaume Beaumier et al., "Global Regulations for a Digital Economy: Between New and Old Challenges," *Policy Insights* 11, no. 4 (2020), https://doi.org/10.1111/1758-5899.12823.

28. Richard Heeks et al., "Digital Platforms and Institutional Voids in Developing Countries: The Case of Ride-Hailing Markets," *World Development* 145 (2021), https://doi.org/https://doi.org/10.1016/j.worlddev.2021.105528.

29. Farinella Domenica and Arcidiacono Davide, "Beyond Formality: The Informalisation and Tertiarisation of Labour in the Gig Economy," in *The Routledge Handbook of the Gig Economy*, ed. Immanuel Ness (London: Routledge, 2022), 116–130.

30. Mark Graham and Mohammad Amir Anwar, "Digital Labour," in *Digital Geographies*, ed. James Ash, Rob Kitchin, and Agnieszka Leszcvynski (London: Sage, 2018).

31. UNHCR, "UNHCR Refugee Data Finder."

32. Hackl, "Key Figure of Mobility," 65.

33. Heeks, "Digital Inequality Beyond the Digital Divide."

34. Jones, *Work Without the Worker*, 11–12.

35. Hackl, "Key Figure of Mobility."

36. Easton-Calabria and Omata, "Panacea for the Refugee Crisis? Rethinking the Promotion of 'Self-Reliance' for Refugees," 1462.

37. Hackl, "Connecting Without Protecting."

38. Easton-Calabria, *Refugees, Self-Reliance, Development: A Critical History*, 195.

39. Easton-Calabria and Omata, "Panacea for the Refugee Crisis? Rethinking the Promotion of 'Self-Reliance' for Refugees," 1462.

40. Hackl, "Connecting Without Protecting."

41. Duffy, "The Romance of Work."

Epilogue

1. GSMA, *Proportionate Regulation in Uganda: A Gateway for Refugees Accessing Mobile Services in Their Own Name* (London: GSMA, 2020), https://www.gsma.com/mobilefordevelopment/resources/proportionate-regulation-in-uganda-a-gateway-for-refugees-accessing-mobile-services-in-their-own-name/.

2. Burton, "'Doing No Harm' in the Digital Age."

3. UNHCR, *Digital Transformation Strategy 2022–2026*.

4. IGF, *Report of the UN Secretary-General's High-level Panel on Digital Cooperation: 2.1 Creating and Incluisve Digital Economy*, High-Level Panel on Digital Cooperation, Internet Governance Forum (2019), https://www.intgovforum.org/multilingual/content/21-creating-an-inclusive-digital-economy.

5. UNCDF, *Inclusive Digital Economies for the SDGs* (New York: UNCDF, 2022), https://www.uncdf.org/ide4sdg; UNCDF, *Inclusive Digital Economies for the SDGs*; UNCDF, *Inclusive Digital Economy Scorecard (IDES) Report—Uganda*.

6. UNHCR, *Digital Transformation Strategy 2022–2026*.

7. UNHCR, *Digital Transformation Strategy 2022–2026*.

8. ILO, *ILO Centenary Declaration for the Future of Work* (Geneva: International Labour Organization, 2019), 3, https://www.ilo.org/media/217791/download.

9. Vicente Silva, "The ILO and the Future of Work: The Politics of Global Labour Policy," *Global Social Policy* 22, no. 2 (2021), https://doi.org/10.1177/14680181211004853.

10. ILO, *ILO Centenary Declaration for the Future of Work*, 7.

11. UNHCR, *Digital Transformation Strategy 2022–2026*, 6.

12. UNHCR, ILO, and UNDP, *Emerging Practices to Improve Access to and Working Conditions on Digital Labour Platforms for Refugees and Host Communities* (2024), https://www.unhcr.org/innovation/wp-content/uploads/2024/10/Emerging-practices-to-improve-access-to-and-working-conditions-on-digital-labour-platforms-for-refugees-and-host-communities---Joint-Report.pdf.

13. UNHCR, ILO, and UNDP, *Emerging Practices to Improve Access to and Working Conditions on Digital Labour Platforms for Refugees and Host Communities*, 32.

14. Hackl, "Connecting Without Protecting."

15. ITU, *Measuring Digital Development*.

16. "Financial Exclusion: The Struggle of Syrian Refugees in Europe," *Social Justice and Accountability Centre*, April 4, 2024, https://syriaaccountability.org/financial-exclusion-the-struggle-of-syrian-refugees-in-europe/.

17. Swati Mehta Dhawan, *Financial Inclusion of Germany's Refugees: Current Situation and Road Ahead*, Working Paper 5, European Microfinance Network (2018), https://www.european-microfinance.org/sites/default/files/document/file/Financial%20Inclusion%20of%20German%20Refugees.pdf.

18. Dhawan and Zollmann, "Financial Inclusion or Encampment?"

19. Casswell, "The Essential Role of Digital Literacy in Contexts of Forced Displacement."

20. Casswell, "The Essential Role of Digital Literacy in Contexts of Forced Displacement."

21. Fairwork, *Fairwork Annual Report 2022* (Fairwork Foundation, 2022), 47, 48, https://fair.work/wp-content/uploads/sites/17/2023/01/Fairwork-Annual-Report-2022_v6_WEB.pdf.

22. Fairwork, *Fairwork Annual Report 2022*, 53.

23. UNHCR, ILO, and UNDP, *Emerging Practices to Improve Access to and Working Conditions on Digital Labour Platforms for Refugees and Host Communities*.

24. Fairwork Europe, *Fairwork's Response to the EU Directive on Platform Work Platforms Should Follow Enforceable Standards!* (2024), https://fair.work/wp-content/uploads/sites/17/2024/03/Fairworks-Response-to-the-EU-Directive-on-Platform-Work.pdf.

25. Martin, *Connecting with Confidence*.

26. Joanna Świątkowska, *Tackling Cybercrime to Unleash Developing Countries' Digital Potential. Background Paper,* Pathways for Prosperity Commission Background Paper Series 33 (Oxford: Pathways for Prosperity Commmission, 2020), 20–22, https://pathwayscommission.bsg.ox.ac.uk/sites/default/files/2020-01/tackling_cybercrime_to_unleash_developing_countries_digital_potential.pdf.

27. Hackl, "Connecting Without Protecting."

28. "Fair Work," accessed June 20, 2023, https://humansintheloop.org/why-us/fair-work-policy/.

29. UNHCR, ILO, and UNDP, *Emerging Practices to Improve Access to and Working Conditions on Digital Labour Platforms for Refugees and Host Communities*, 12.

30. Shuting Xia and Lorraine Charles, *Digital Employment Pipelines for Refugees: A Systematic Review* (Jobtech Alliance and Na'amal, 2025), https://jobtechalliance.com/wp-content/uploads/2025/04/Digital-Employment-Pipelines-for-Refugees-2025.pdf?utm_source=PDF&utm_medium=Blog&utm_campaign=Report+digital+employment+refugees&utm_id=Digital+Employment+Pipelines+for+Refugees%3A+A+Systematic+Review.

31. MIT Open Learning, "Empowering Talent, Strengthening Businesses: The Opportunities of Impact Outsourcing—MS 2024," Migration Summit 2024, YouTube, July 10 2024, https://www.youtube.com/watch?v=1Oc8k6DNQ3k&list=PL6cp6kydiOXcS3y4_vumcYg6jJZQSHF8y&index=5.

32. MIT Open Learning, "Empowering Talent, Strengthening Businesses."

33. MIT Open Learning, "Empowering Talent."

34. MIT Open Learning, "Empowering Talent."

35. ILO, *World Employment and Social Outlook*, 82.

36. Fairwork, *Fairwork Cloudwork Ratings 2023*.

37. Kelle Howson et al., "Stripping Back the Mask: Working Conditions on Digital Labour Platforms During the Covid-19 Pandemic," *International Labour Review*, 161, no. 3 (2022): 437.

38. iWorkers, "About," https://iworkers.co/about-us/.

39. ILO PROSPECTS, *Review of National Policy, Legislative and Regulatory Frameworks and Practice*, 62.

Index

Publisher contact:
The MIT Press
Massachusetts Institute of Technology
77 Massachusetts Avenue, Cambridge, MA 02139
mitpress.mit.edu

EU Authorised Representative:
Easy Access System Europe, Mustamäe tee 50,
10621 Tallinn, Estonia
gpsr.requests@easproject.com

Printed by Integrated Books International,
United States of America